Meetings that Work

A Practical Guide

to Teamworking

in groups

Catherine Widdicombe

The Lutterworth Press
Cambridge

The short extract from Vincent J Donovan, *Christianity Rediscovered* © SCM Press 1978 is used by permission.

Every effort has been made to trace the copyright holders of material used in this book. Any inadvertent infringement will be corrected in future reprints.

The Lutterworth Press
P.O. Box 60
Cambridge
CB1 2NT
England

e-mail: **publishing@lutterworth.com**
website: **http://www.lutterworth.com**

ISBN 0 7188 xxxx x

British Library Cataloguing in Publication Data:
A catalogue record is available from the British Library.

© Catherine Widdicombe, 1994, 2000

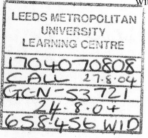
Typeset by Tukan, High Wycombe

Printed by Redwood Books

To my mother
to whom I owe so much

Never accept and be content with unanalyzed assumptions, assumptions about the work, about the people, about the Church or Christianity. Never be afraid to ask questions about the works we have inherited or the work we are doing. There is no question that should not be asked or that is outlawed. The day we are completely satisfied with what we have been doing; the day we have found the perfect unchangeable system of work, the perfect answer, never in need of being corrected again, on that day we will know that we are wrong, that we have made the greatest mistake of all.

Vincent J. Donovan

CONTENTS

ACKNOWLEDGEMENTS

My manifold indebtedness to George Lovell is acknowledged in the Introduction. He has been a loyal, supportive and creatively critical colleague, mentor and friend. It was he who first suggested that I write this book. My gratitude to him for all he has given me can never be adequately acknowledged or repaid. Another person without whom this book would never have been written is T.R. Batten. Meeting him first in the written word and then in person led me to develop the understanding and skills I was searching for at a major moment of transition in my life. He has encouraged and stood by me ever since. I am deeply thankful to God that both of them have been part of my life.

I am also grateful to all those who have been my colleagues and co-workers over the years. They are too numerous to mention by name but I well recall the first, John V. Budd, who, in accepting an invitation to coffee, took on a co-learning colleagueship which started me practising non-directive group work. Only I am aware of – and surely do not appreciate fully – the patience and forbearance my colleagues down the years have exercised in my regard. Not only with them but from them I have learnt much.

To members of all the hundreds of groups I have ever worked with, I say thank you. Many will never read or know of my gratitude. They have taught me much as we struggled to think, wrestled with problems, overcame crises, faced many an impasse or backed out of cul-de-sacs. Good humour, commitment, confusion, frustration, anger and excitement are among the many ingredients which have been part of such relationships. From all I have learnt.

I am also indebted to those who have read, criticised and improved my manuscripts: above all this includes Margaret Brown who has given many hours of detailed work and been constantly encouraging as well as challenging. My thanks also go to those who have typed and checked the numerous drafts, particularly May Farina and Irene Picton who were endlessly and cheerfully patient.

Lastly, I thank my Grail community which over the years has given me the freedom to follow the strong call I felt to Church and Community Development work, out of which the present book has been forged. Despite misgivings and puzzlement in the early days, they have been generous in their support, spiced as it was with the necessary element of challenge. I am deeply grateful: only I know what this has meant to me.

INTRODUCTION

In the Western world we have a plethora of groups and meetings. From multi-national businesses to enclosed religious orders, from professional bodies and statutory services to church and community groups, from teams of colleagues to training courses, from bible study to self-help therapy. People depend largely on meeting together to keep things going and to move things forward. "Not another meeting!" is a sad reflection on the quality of many meetings. They are too often experienced as deadening rather than lifegiving. This book is written in the conviction that group meetings, teams and committees of all sorts have a potential both for development and enjoyment which is seldom realised.

Meetings that Work as a title needs some explanation. What sort of meetings are being addressed? The word meeting as I am using it, refers to a gathering of people met together with a task to do which entails the exchange of thoughts and feelings. Simply said but enormously complex.

The task of a group or team may include such things as planning and organising work or research of one kind or another; thinking more deeply about some subject such as racism or religion; learning a skill or giving mutual support. Its task may concern solely the members within the group or it may be to do with others beyond its bounds, as for instance, a staff meeting or a business team which has to relate to a complex system of groups and organisations both locally and nationally. What is written is both about how to help people work at the task and about engendering the kind of interpersonal relationships which will enable them to do so.

Groups may be temporary or long-term; new or established; large or small. Teams may be autonomous or part of a larger organisation. Their meetings may be more or less formal or informal. Groups such as committees, councils, boards, and professional associations will operate at a more formal level than groups such as fellowships, community or church groups, those focussing on a specific issue such as justice and peace, or catering for particular people, youth, young mothers, or the elderly. Many firms are now setting up interdisciplinary teams concerned with new developments and which, for greater effectiveness, need to work in an informal collaborative style rather than in a more formal hierarchical mode.

Groups may have a permanent or rotating chairperson or facilitator who may be self-chosen, elected by the members or appointed by the organisation. The members may be elected or co-opted, their membership may be voluntary, expected or compulsory. The group may be part of their work life or their leisure. Attendance may be regular or fluid. They may or may not have a shared history reaching into the past. They are likely to bring to a meeting a variety of personal needs and concerns, many of which will never be openly acknowledged. These may be connected with the group or completely separate from it, something in their private life which is preoccupying them. Clearly, the task of making a meeting work is complex and challenging.

This book is not primarily written for purely social or fellowship groups at one end of the spectrum nor for formal committees at the other, but for that wide range of groups in which people meet to do a task and want to work at that task more systematically and creatively.

All such groups and teams, whatever their degree of autonomy, and they vary widely, experience certain constraints, internal or external, which reduce their freedom to act. These may be established by custom, tradition, legal requirements, or the situation in which they find themselves. But however binding the constraints, as for instance, committees with their constitutions, procedures, given purposes or tasks, the members always retain a degree of freedom to think and pursue that for which the group was formed. This book is about ways and means of helping groups of people to think, discuss and act together within that area of freedom which is theirs, or to use it to question and push out the boundaries if they decide they cannot work effectively within them.

It is written for anyone who wants to help people in a meeting of any kind to work together in a collaborative way, believing that individuals, groups and communities flourish when people have a say in decisions which affect them.

It is about how to help a group or team function better. It is not about the subject matter which people meet to discuss. For instance, it includes hints on how to deal with faction in a meeting but it does not consider how to work with conflict in the neighbourhood or society.

Although its focus is not on formal committees, I know from my experience of discussing with many people, that much of what I have written here is applicable and could be easily adapted by those working with committees. It is desirable with all task centred groups that their meetings are characterised by creative thinking, open and critical exploration of ideas, and the kind of participation in which all contributions and people are taken seriously.

Most of what is written focuses on meetings of between eight and twenty members although there is a section on working with large groups and much of what is written applies to meetings of all sizes.

This book draws on over twenty-five years experience of helping people with little or no training in group work skills, to conduct the sort of meetings which promote the development of participants, individually and collectively. By development I mean the process whereby people become more thoughtful and self-determining and more sensitively aware of their responsibilities towards others.

Since 1972 there has been a close working partnership between George Lovell and myself as we have worked with groups and communities in the church and neighbourhood in Project 70-75 and in Avec, an agency in church and community work. So many of his ideas have become part of me, that I hardly know where his work ends and mine begins. I remain responsible for the formulation of ideas in this book although drawing heavily on his work and thinking. Where I have used his notes I have written sometimes in my own words, sometimes in his, sometimes in a mixture with a view to putting things as clearly as possible and so that things fit together and flow. Where, for one reason or another, it is clear that I am using his work, it is acknowledged.

The subject matter arises from the difficulties which people faced in conducting meetings and because of which they sought help from Avec. It is based on an appreciation of the essential use of the non-directive approach as defined by T.R. Batten in *The Non-Directive Approach in Group and Community Work.*[1] This book limits itself to the practical application of the non-directive approach in meetings.

Avec was a Christian and ecumenical agency and therefore some of the examples, but by no means all, come from Christian groups. Howbeit, as every group or team, however unique, shares in a common humanity, I believe that what one learns from working with one group, wherever it is set, can be relevant to many other meetings and situations.

Using this book

If you are responsible for running a meeting and want to help the members to function more effectively, this book is written for you. It aims to engender in you, as group worker or facilitator, an attitude and a habit of open and critical questioning about what you are doing, why you are doing it, and how you could do it more effectively. It is not a set of rules or a blue print for success.

Just as every team leader is unique, and every group is unique, so is the relationship between them. There may be common problems but individual solutions have to be worked out. Techniques alone will not suffice. The heart of the matter is to do with your attitudes and beliefs: hence the success of this book is bound up closely with promoting an inner dialogue in you, the reader. For this reason I have made an extensive use of questions. Questions are thought-provoking. I believe that questions will draw upon the mine of information and insights you have gained from the experience of living and working and meeting with people at home, and in school, work and neighbourhood.

It is therefore a book to be used as you work rather than to be read from start to finish. It is a reference book: use the extended list of contents and the index to search for what you need, whether you are starting a group, working with people you know or do not know, wanting to develop a particular skill, facing a problem, wanting to promote participation or engage in a decision-making process. As appropriate, summaries and check lists are included as an aid to its practical use.

The shape of this book

All groups have a starting point. For some this may be lost in the realms of history. For others it may be a more recent remembered event. As a facilitator you may join an existing group or you may want or be asked to start one. Once started, many groups have a chequered career, with stops and re-starts, or convene so infrequently that each meeting has some of the characteristics of a new group. Furthermore, groups are changed as members come and go. This can be a gradual process or it may be experienced as a sudden transformation or a new beginning.

PART ONE, therefore, is about establishing a new group and its re-establishment after periods of inactivity or infrequent meetings and it includes a section on the welcoming of new members, and organising a one-off meeting.

Every meeting, whether it is a one-off or one of a series of meetings, has a beginning, a middle and an end; it also has a before and an after.

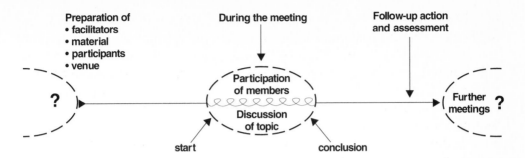

As a group worker thinking ahead to a meeting you have several complementary goals to keep in mind. Your purpose is a fundamental touchstone to guide your thinking: what changes for the better are you hoping to achieve in the lives of this group of people? The quality of the meeting depends in large part on the quality and care of the preparatory thought which has gone into it and this begins with the preparation done by you as facilitator. Fundamental to this preparation is the consideration of people's emotions, expectations, motives and willingness to participate in the meeting; their individual attitudes and relationships to each other, to you, and to the wider group or community; and the task of the group and the objectives of the meeting.

PART TWO is therefore to do with what happens before a meeting: the preparation of the group worker, of the material, of the participants and of the venue. Thorough preparation for a meeting takes time. It is therefore not feasible to prepare in depth for all meetings. It can be important to decide on the crucial meetings for which you will prepare thoroughly and just how much preparation you need to do to ensure that other meetings are profitable.

PART THREE deals with the conduct of a meeting and the interaction of members with each other and with the facilitator at the start, during the actual discussion, and at the conclusion. During the meeting aim to ensure that the objectives for the meeting are successfully achieved; promote participation of an open and critical kind in which people grapple with ideas together in a co-operative and creative way; and get ideas worked at clearly and systematically, seriously and realistically. Clearly what has been discussed by way of preparation is relevant here also. Hence I include detailed cross references to indicate the relationship between the preparatory planning and the actual conduct of the meeting.

PART FOUR discusses possible action after and between meetings.

PART FIVE considers some common situations and problems.

PART SIX deals with specific application of the above ideas to groups of different kinds and particular situations.

PART SEVEN is about developing one's own and other people's group work skills.

As this book has grown from all I have learnt from so many people, I would like to continue the process by requesting you, the reader, to send in comments or insights, problems or questions for incorporation should a third edition be published.

Catherine Widdicombe
August 1999

A note about terminology

- As the English language does not have unisex pronouns I have alternated the use of 'he' and 'she' as appropriate.

- The term 'group worker' or facilitator is used rather than group or team leader, which smacks of giving an authoritarian or directive lead, or chair-person, as this could imply only more formal groups and committees.

NOTE

1. T.R. Batten in collaboration with Madge Batten, *The Non-Directive Approach in Group and Community Work* (Oxford University Press 1967). Abridged version, *The Non-Directive Approach* (An Avec Publication 1990).

PART ONE

Establishing and re-establishing a group

Groups are formed in a variety of ways: a committee sets up a working party and people volunteer or are invited to join it; an individual decides to set up a group, for example, a youth worker starts a group for young people; a number of people together decide to have regular meetings about justice and peace issues; or a new staff team is formed, and so on.

If you find yourself in this kind of situation, thinking through the points below will enable you to alert people to questions and issues which need to be considered as you plan, recruit, organise, and start a new group. If you are starting from scratch it can be immensely supportive to find someone who will partner you in the enterprise.

I. ESTABLISHING A NEW GROUP

1. Conditions for success

Groups are more likely to get off to a good start if:
- the purpose and underlying philosophy of the group is clear from the start or is clarified early on;
- people join freely and not because they are pressurised to join. They may need to be encouraged and motivated but this is different from exerting undue pressure. People need to be given time to think about joining, possibly experience a few meetings, and decide for themselves whether or not it is for them;
- the practicalities are decided upon together so that they fit the various needs of all the members. It did not help the cause of a woman in South London who wanted to set up a group on ecology when she said "the group must meet within walking distance of my home". Not surprisingly there was a minimal response;
- the way the group is to be run is clarified and agreed from the beginning: some people may want to be in a group where everyone actively participates; others may do so much discussing and deciding at work that they seek a group where they are the recipients in one way or another;
- the life span of the group is clear: it may be for a specific period, to do a specific job, or be indefinite. If the latter, it can be useful to build in a review after so many meetings or months;
- it is clear to what people are and are not committing themselves in terms of frequency of meetings, time, effort, finance, etc.;
- the group sets itself realistic and limited objectives.

2. Recruiting initial members

Where applicable, the way in which a group is recruited effects its ongoing life. The following areas could well be considered.

- *Involving people in the process:* The more people who actively participate, the wider the net is likely to be. However, the approximate size of the group needs to be decided: this and the nature of the group will determine who to involve. A more intimate type of group will not want to attract too many people. Some of the methods outlined on page 29 may be used.

- *Criteria for membership:* The basic criteria may suggest themselves by the nature of the group and include such things as "interested in, agreed about and committed to x, able and willing to attend meetings regularly", as well as more obvious factors such as age, sex, denomination, skills and abilities, responsibilities, job, qualifications, location, etc. There may be other criteria which refer to the group as a whole, for instance, the balance between the sexes, races, or denominations; a wide variety of complementary skills and abilities; people from different firms, departments, organisations, areas or communities and so on.

- *Publicity:* Any publicity needs to reflect the ethos of the group and state its aims as clearly as possible, thus enabling the self-selection of members. However, you may decide against an open invitation in case it attracts inappropriate people. In either case a personal invitation is likely to be more effective, whether it be in face-to-face conversation, by phone or in a letter.

3. Launching: the first meeting

A new group will not immediately start functioning at full capacity. Time and patience are needed before people settle down, feel at ease with each other, and work out an acceptable *modus vivendi.* One way of describing the early history of a new group is in terms of four overlapping stages through which many groups go:

Forming: Members begin to get to know each other and to see what different people, including themselves, have to contribute to the group.

Storming: People become more familiar and underlying disparities and tensions are liable to surface, as individuals try to establish their place in the group and how they can make a contribution. Differences of opinion, expectations, ideas and assumptions, brought from other groups and situations, have to be worked through.

Norming: Gradually a way of operating as a group becomes generally accepted and agreed.

Performing: The group is now ready to work together and tackle more exacting tasks.

The first meeting is important in getting the group off to a good start. Your own welcoming attitude is key and much of what is written about preparing yourself for a meeting is relevant here (p. 35).

Introductions: Those who arrive for the meeting need to feel not only welcomed by you but at ease with each other. Having an informal cup of coffee as people gather can be helpful. Introductions can be simple or elaborate, serious or hilarious. Choose a method which is in keeping with the subject matter and nature of the meeting: this will set the tone and atmosphere and colour people's expectations. It can be useful for each member to say something by way of introduction, even if it is only their name and where they come from. It helps them to speak again. Or they might be asked to say why they are at the meeting, what attracted them to it, or what they are hoping to get out of it. Unnecessary time may be taken up or people become restless if some members talk for too long. You may prevent this by asking people for "only two or three sentences". Alternatively you may suggest people talk to their neighbour and then ask them to introduce each other to the group. If you are able to take longer over the introductions you could ask people informally to spend a couple of minutes talking to every person.

On the other hand, if time is at a premium, it can be useful after the briefest of introductions, to get on with the business of the meeting but early on, ask people to talk in twos or threes in response to a question on what you have been saying. Such early use of buzz groups can help individuals to feel relaxed and involved. The arrival of a latecomer can provide a useful opportunity to get people to repeat their names, and for you to summarise what has been said so far: many people will not have taken everything in and be glad of the repetition (p. 89).

II. RE-ESTABLISHING A GROUP

For a variety of reasons a group may need to be re-established. It may be that after a long summer break or planned period of inactivity the group simply re-convenes; or it could be that after a crisis, a period of stagnation or dwindling membership, a new start becomes necessary. In this case people are more likely to put their heart into this if they see it as an opportunity to build on what was good in the past and avoid some of the pitfalls. Much of what has been written about starting up a new group (p. 25) will be applicable.

In either case people will need time to re-establish their relationships. After a break, there will be news which they want to share and time may need to be allowed for this. It may be done informally or in a structured way, for instance, by asking each one to share one item of news or something which is on their mind, or say how they feel about returning to the group. Decide what would best fit your group.

A re-start provides an opportunity to look again at the aims of the group, to check them out and amend or revise them. In the same way practicalities can be re-considered: the frequency, time and place of meetings; the way of working together or tackling the task; and the plan or programme for the coming months.

It may be appropriate to review the past in a more detailed way (p. 126). What do people feel went well in the group? What was helpful? Why did they come or what did they get from the group? What do people feel needs changing? Were there things they disliked or felt uneasy about? Why did people stop coming? Are there any new ideas and suggestions which could be discussed?

In discussing these things it is important to remember that the group belongs to everyone, facilitator and members: everyone has a responsibility to make a success of it. Time spent in openly discussing these things and making arrangements which are mutually convenient is time well spent. No one should be made to feel guilty if everything did not work out well in the past. The great value of things going wrong is the learning opportunity this provides. One rarely goes down the same blind alley twice.

III. RECRUITING AND WELCOMING NEW MEMBERS

Some groups, such as working parties, are formed for a specific purpose and have a limited life with a stable membership. Others, such as tenants' associations, are on-going and may need to recruit members; in others, new members may automatically join on becoming a new member of staff or of a residential community.

Groups may be variously open or closed, they may consciously or unconsciously encourage or discourage new recruits, and make it easy or difficult for people to join them and to feel at home in them. Most people, although they adopt various devices to cloak it, find approaching and joining a new group something of an ordeal. Potential members may become committed from their first meeting; or decide on a trial period of several meetings; or simply attend a few meetings and then decide whether or not to remain.

It is important to remember that one or more new members change the shape of a group: it may have the same name, members may subscribe to the same purpose, continue to do what they have always done, but in fact, a new and different group of people is meeting together. The group may be enriched by an influx of new insights and abilities but there may well be difficulties in being open to them and integrating the newcomers.

This section considers what the facilitator and group can do in relation to recruiting new members, preparing for them, and integrating them into the group.

1. **Recruiting new members**

There are several related questions below from which you could pick appropriately to help a group to consider recruitment:

- *Attitudes towards recruitment*. Do we want new members? Are we ready for them now or do we need first to get better established or know each other better? Should we actively recruit or wait for people to turn up? Are there specific times when it would be easier than others to absorb new members (e.g., at the end of a cycle of work rather than half way through)? Do we need to recruit regularly so the group will continue as members leave for various reasons? For example, a group responsible for a job in the community or an organisation would be wise to encourage younger members and train them so they are able to carry on the work as people retire from age, ill-health or leave the area.

- *Criteria for membership*. Some groups by their very nature are open to anyone, others are for specific people. Is anyone welcome to join the group? If not, what are the criteria? What sort of people are we looking for (p. 26)?

- *Methods of recruiting*. How can we make ourselves known so people can respond appropriately? Some of these suggestions may be of use:
  - have an 'open meeting' at which the function and activities of the group are explained and displayed;
  - issue an open invitation through the organisation's outlets (written in newsletters or magazines or spoken about at a function or gathering) or through a local press advertisement for community groups;

- list all the groups and agencies and people who might be approached. Ask the group to brainstorm their ideas. Brainstorming works best if certain 'rules' are adhered to (p. 98);
  - using registers and lists, review by name everyone in the locality known to members to decide who to invite to the group.

2. Preparing for new members

The group worker may need to help members prepare for newcomers by considering their own feelings and what new members may feel.

The feelings of the current group members: When a group has been together for some time it can be difficult to be genuine in welcoming newcomers. Members may need to discuss how they feel and find ways of dealing with any negative feelings they have. Some of the suggestions as to how as facilitator you could deal with your negative emotions (p. 42) could be adapted or adopted.

The feelings of new members: Since everyone will have experienced being new to a group, it may well be that no more is needed than a word to alert people beforehand as to how new members may feel when they come along to their first meeting. If, however, it is a close knit group which no one has joined for some time it may be useful to do one or more of the following:
  - discuss together how they will welcome and assimilate new members and who will do what;
  - take the members on a journey of remembrance, thinking about a particular group they joined or failed to join and recalling their feelings and what helped and hindered their integration (p. 73);
  - get members to stand in the shoes of the potential new members and imagine how they are feeling and what they may be thinking and expecting (p. 74);
  - list what would help new people to feel welcome or unwelcome; what they need to know about the group: the members, the mores, procedures, history, purpose, etc.

3. Integrating new members

What is done to prepare potential new members before their first meeting and to welcome them to it, will depend very much on the nature of the group, its ethos, the degree of formality or informality, its circumstances, and whether a newcomer is expected or just turns up.

Before their first meeting: Among the possibilities by way of preparing new-comers beforehand the group may want to consider such things as:

- sending information through the post: this could be a letter of information, a descriptive brochure or booklet, the constitutions, trust deed, records or minutes of previous meetings or a welcoming note. What is likely to inform without overwhelming someone? What will make them feel wanted without putting undue pressure on them?

- an informal contact giving opportunity for questions to be asked and information given. This could be a telephone call or a meeting with one or more members.

- arranging for one of the group to bring the new members along to their first meeting.

- inviting new members to a preliminary social occasion or some group event.

At their first meeting: In deciding how best to help one or more new people to feel welcome and to become integrated into the group, members could ask themselves such questions as:

- Are they likely to find it easiest to receive a quiet word of welcome and to be allowed to spend their first meeting or two quietly observing and getting the feel of things?

- Would it help if we had some sort of celebration before or after the meeting: for example, something to eat or drink informally?

- How can we get to know each other? Would it be best done gradually as we discuss and work together or should we each introduce ourselves? If the latter, with how much detail? (p. 27)

- How can we give the new members some idea of the history, ethos and purpose of the group? Have we any reports, visual aids, photographs, or videos which would be a useful introduction?

- Do we expect them to pick up the procedures as we go along or are there certain things they need to know from the start?

- How can we encourage them to participate without pressurising them? How can we be open to their ideas and contributions?

- Would it help if one of the group keeps an eye on or befriends each new member?

- How can we ensure they understand, agree with and are committed to the basic philosophy and purpose of the group? Do we foresee any danger of newcomers wanting to steer the group in a new direction? How could we deal with this? What is negotiable/non-negotiable?

IV. SETTING UP A ONE-OFF MEETING

Much time and effort can be put into organising a meeting for which a disappointing few turn up. Unless people are under compulsion to attend, this will at times be inevitable, but asking oneself certain questions beforehand may help to ensure that it happens less frequently.

1. **The purpose of the meeting**

The purpose or objective of a meeting is closely connected with the question of who you want to attend. As well as categories of people, such as parents or local residents, consider their attitude or frame of mind. Presumably, you are hoping for people who will take a real interest, benefit and contribute, rather than be likely to misunderstand, be bored or pour scorn.

2. **Encouraging appropriate participants**

Learn from your own experience. Try working through the points below as you think about your own response to the possibility of attending various meetings. It might help to make a check list as you do so.

What makes you want to attend or decide against going to a meeting?

There may be several interrelated factors in relation to:

- what you think and feel about the person or group setting up the meeting or where you saw it advertised.

- the way in which the invitation or advertisement is couched and presented: the tone of voice, over enthusiasm or lack of it, the amount of pressure, print, illustrations, etc.

- the subject matter: You are likely to be influenced by whether or not the topic concerns, interests or intrigues you, or is likely to benefit you.

- your situation, for instance the time factor: you may be overstretched, or have time on your hands, be feeling bored or low and welcome an opportunity to get out of the house. Attending may entail complicated arrangements for transport or baby-sitter and not be worth the effort or expense.

  For further suggestions see *Convening a Meeting* (p. 79).

Finally, it is worth testing the way you intend to present the invitation on one or two people whom you hope will attend.

PART TWO

Before a meeting

The major factors to be considered when preparing to work with a group are outlined below. Where appropriate a short checklist is appended after sections but you could devise your own checklists, taking into account your own style of working and unique situation. It is wise to prepare for a meeting some days in advance so that ideas have time to mature and be reconsidered after a lapse of time.

Developing a routine of preparation which suits you is an important factor in motivating you to do it. The questions below may help you to establish such a routine.

When to prepare? Some people only feel secure if their preparation is done well in advance. Others claim they cannot get inspired until the meeting is almost upon them. Preparing thoroughly too long in advance has the danger of the material becoming stale for you. Leaving things to the last moment may mean you do not have time to look up information you suddenly realise you need, or think through issues which emerge late in the day. Try to find the happy mean for you, maintaining the freshness of the subject and allowing you to check your preparation and have second – and even third – thoughts.

Another aspect is the time of day. Are you a lark with all your most creative work done early or an owl who works late into the night?

Where to prepare? Find a venue and situation which attracts you to the task. Which of the following would help: a clear table top? an armchair? being alone? silence? background music? putting your feet up? being outdoors? walking?

What to use? Some people work on paper, others work in their heads, and others use a typewriter or computer. The paper, whether lined or not, and its colour can effect you. At times a pencil is wanted, at others a pen. Such seemingly unimportant things can make a great difference to one's motivation.

Clearly not every meeting can be or needs to be prepared for in the detail outlined below. All meetings are likely to benefit if you prepare thoroughly for key meetings.

I. PREPARING YOURSELF FOR A MEETING

1. Thinking about your attitudes and values

As human beings our basic beliefs and values, whatever they may be, affect and inform our attitudes and the way that we treat ourselves and other people. Much of this may be subconscious and yet greatly affect our outlook and behaviour. The more aware we are of what we believe and value, the more control we can exert over the formation of our attitudes.

Have you ever asked yourself what helps you to function your best as a group worker? For me, my own attitudes and deeply held beliefs exert a strong influence on my feelings and this affects how I operate. What I believe about people and their ability to enter into creative thinking and discussion with others and come to good decisions, and what I believe about myself and my ability to stimulate this process, will influence my approach to the group and will communicate itself in subtle and intangible ways. It will also affect my overt behaviour.

I suggest therefore that an important part of your preparation is to reflect on your beliefs, values and assumptions which colour your attitude towards yourself and others. If they are inconsistent with those underlying the approaches advocated in this book, then much of what is written will jar or be of little use to you. It is necessary therefore at this stage, for me to spell out the key beliefs and assumptions about people and their well-being, on which I have based the approaches and methods suggested in this book. Is there congruence between those below and your own?

CREDO . . .

I believe as human beings we are more alive when we use our minds to think openly and critically about our experience, our situation, information we receive, events which occur, other people and ourselves, including our feelings about these things. The approaches and methods suggested here are designed to stimulate people to think: to think about their own ideas and feelings and the ideas and feelings of other people including myself as facilitator. I see this as an important part of the life-long process of development.

Furthermore and flowing from this, I believe people have a unique and valuable contribution to make to decisions which affect them, and that generally speaking, they are in a better position to make good decisions about their lives than I am. I believe, nevertheless, that people are able to give, and often need to receive, help from others in order to make good decisions for themselves. The non-directive approach, as conceived by T.R. Batten[1] offers this help without in any way making decisions for another person.

What I believe about others I believe about myself. I may have valuable insights and useful ideas to contribute to a decision making process or to an individual or a group, but I do not have all the answers. In relation to groups, I believe in maximising the combined resources, the wealth of experience, ideas and insights of all the members in order to reach wise conclusions and achieve decisions which have everyone's backing.

(2) Clarifying and deciding upon your approach[2]

The approach advocated in this book is called 'non-directive' and despite its negative-sounding description, it is in fact a very positive approach, as will be seen from the following outline of the functions of non-directive facilitators. Their aim is to work with the members of a group, to help them think clearly and systematically about what they wish to think about in relation to the purpose of the group. In order to do this they:

* *Create an atmosphere in which members feel free to speak*

  Ensure that everyone is comfortable and in a position to see and hear everyone else. Caring for people's needs in this way helps to reassure them that they will be accepted and supported. You may need to devise ways of helping shy members to speak if they wish to (p. 136); of preventing one or two dominating the group (p. 138); in short, of allowing everyone to contribute. Get minority views considered.

* *Get agreement about the topic to be discussed*

  Clarify the task of the group (p. 88) and ensure that members are agreed on precisely what they are going to discuss. This will entail reaching initial agreement on what to discuss and testing to make sure it is genuine. This is discussed under 'Testing questions' on page 58.

  Help members to keep to the point they have decided to discuss. For example, when discussion wanders, say so and ask whether members want to return to their original line or consciously choose the new one (p. 100).

* *Get clarity in the discussion*

  Ensure members are clear about just what is being talked about as the discussion proceeds.

  Help members to clarify their contributions if for any reason they are unclear.

Listen and help others to listen until they really understand what is being said (people often argue against each other because they are not clear about what the other person is saying).

Indicate any major differences of opinion within the group (as these become apparent) and encourage members to investigate why they differ rather than argue for their respective views (p. 144).

- *Get all points of view considered objectively whatever you personally may think or feel* (p. 43)

Do not ask loaded questions (e.g., "Don't you think that . . ."?).

Do not take sides when members disagree but get the areas of disagreement explored openly and objectively.

Contribute your own ideas as appropriate. This is discussed on page 90.

- *Summarise the discussion*

Summarise briefly at appropriate times to help members to see what progress has been made so far and what further areas still need to be explored. This helps to catch up anyone who has got left behind and it focuses the thinking of the group. (For more detailed exploration see *'Summarising and Conceptualising'* p. 110.)

- *Provide relevant information*

Enable people to participate in a discussion and help a group to take account of as many factors as possible by feeding in information and ideas as necessary or appropriate. Doing this as objectively as you can ensures that such information and ideas are considered as openly and critically as those of other people (p. 91).

- *Structure the discussion* (p. 49)

Help members to think systematically, e.g., to discuss a problem before jumping to solutions.

Try to put the points which arise in some sort of relationship to each other or to clarify any emerging pattern.

- *Ask questions rather than make statements*

Questions stimulate thought and are therefore a key tool when using the non-directive approach (p. 55).

Having clarified the approach of a non-directive group worker, consider *your* customary way of conducting meetings. How does your style compare with the general approach and specific aspects outlined above? Does this way of working attract you sufficiently to make you want to have a go? If so, practice and learning from your experience is called for. No one ever achieves perfection as a facilitator: becoming increasingly effective depends on training yourself as you work. If you are new to this approach and wish to work in this way, see *'Beginning to work in a new way'* (p. 183) and *'On going self-training'* (p. 190).

(3.) Your feelings about the group and the meeting

However laudable and altruistic our underlying attitudes and beliefs, we are likely from time to time to experience feelings which may cause us to treat people in a way at variance with our values and purposes, by appearing critical or judgmental or overwhelming people with our feelings of excitement and enthusiasm. In the section below there are suggestions to help you, first, to recall what you know about the group with which you will be working; second, to reflect on your feelings in relation to the group and the meeting; and third, to decide on any action you need to take to prevent your feelings having a negative effect on the group.

Recall what you know about the group. You may know a group well, not at all, or by hearsay. Knowledge of a group can be helpful but it can also be inhibiting. Recalling what you know may alert you to information which you need to find out. It can also alert you to difficulties you may come up against in your own feelings or in the group and enable you to prepare for or pre-empt them.

With groups with which you are familiar, you are likely to know more than you think you know and to find more relevance in your knowledge than you expect. It is useful to recall and consider anything which is part of or contributes to the current life of the group. This may include facts and feelings, attitudes and expectations, past history and future hopes, the present situation, and members' ability or lack of it to think about and analyse their situation and its context. Because of the importance of a particular meeting you may want to take some time doing this or you may only need to give yourself ten minutes or so to get out the key features which strike you. Writing things down and drawing diagrams may clarify and order the information you have (p. 70). The following questions or tasks may be helpful:

- What are the characteristics of this group?

- Are there any particular factors I need to take into account: size, venue, practices, etc.?

- How do members feel or how do I think they feel about themselves and the meeting? Are they likely to be committed to the task? What are their probable expectations, fears, feelings, etc.?

- What do I know of their past history? Are they used to thinking and discussing openly together?

- Are there likely to be any concerns or relationships which will affect the meeting but which may not be made overt, any 'hidden' agenda?

- Have I any clues as to what the group thinks and feels about me and my way of working? How do members see me? Do they stereotype me in any way?

- What are my relationships with different members of the group? Could any of these cause difficulties?

- Work out the advantages and disadvantages of working with a group which knows you well. Raising your awareness may help you to ameliorate the disadvantages and build on the advantages.

- How do the members normally operate in the group? What are the relationships between them? For instance, are members likely to listen to some more than others? Are some individuals stereotyped: the clown, the dominating person, the silent member, the argumentative, etc.?

- What are the likely expectations of the members? What might they be expecting from me, from the meeting, from the group? Are their expectations likely to be similar, to differ significantly, to be realistic, to be appropriate, have major negative or positive effects on me, on themselves, or on others? Are their expectations likely to be helpful and motivating, challenging, cause difficulties? If so, of what sort? What do their expectations stem from? Problems caused by conflicting expectations are discussed on page 78, '*Orientation and prior thought*'.

Reflect on your feelings: One or other of the following suggestions may help you to become aware of your attitude and feelings towards a particular group or meeting and their possible negative effects. Try to be as open as possible.

- Sit quiet and relaxed with paper and pen. Picture the setting in which you will meet the group, think about the members and the meeting for which you are preparing. Imagine being with them. What do you feel as you anticipate the meeting? Jotting down your positive and negative feelings, your expectations, your hopes, concerns, worries, etc., will help you to objectify them.

- Ask a colleague or friend to give you half an hour to listen to you and ask questions to help you explore how you feel about the forthcoming meeting. You need someone whom you trust and who will accept your feelings rather than be judgmental in any way.

- List the possible good and bad effects of your feelings in relation to what you hope to achieve with the group.

- Think about the group and see if a symbol comes to mind. If it does, explore it and reflect on it and see what it is saying to you about your feelings towards the group (p. 109).

- Ask yourself questions, for instance:

    How do I foresee my relationship with them?

    Are they the sort of people I am accustomed to working with or do I feel I may experience difficulty in getting on their wavelength or keeping up with them intellectually?

    How do I feel about the members of the group, as individuals and as a whole?

    Are there any members I feel particularly apprehensive about?

    Why am I feeling apprehensive?

    Do I foresee any specific difficulties?

Decide what action to take: Owning your feelings is a first step in coming to terms with them and deciding how to avoid or ameliorate any potentially unhelpful effects they could have on you or the group and the relationship between you. Further steps may be taken on your own or with a friend or colleague or with the group itself. There may be some things you can do beforehand, some things you can do at the start of the meeting, and others you can do as the meeting is in progress. Some of the suggestions below could be useful on various occasions, others are more specific:

In relation to feelings in general

- Enlist the help of a colleague, alert her to your feelings and the potentially harmful effects on the meeting or group, and ask her to help you during the meeting to avoid them.

- Remind yourself that there may be others in the group with similar feelings and part of your task is to help them make their contribution in the best possible way.

- Look back on past experiences when you felt the same way and ask yourself if your present feelings are exacerbated by them. Analysing the reasons behind your feelings may help you to come to terms with them.

- Remind yourself of times when your expectations have proved alarmist. Realising that expectations are liable to be self-fulfilling prophecies, try to cultivate more hopeful and positive ones.

When feeling nervous and inadequate

One's self-confidence or lack of it results to some extent from past experiences, many of which are lost to conscious memory. As a facilitator my attitude towards myself is of critical importance, and with all of us, this is likely to fluctuate: at times we feel nervous and inadequate and at others we feel confident. I find it important to boost my self-confidence so that I go into a meeting with a hopeful expectation of a good outcome.[3] The suggestions below may help you.

- Remind yourself that there are valuable resources in the group, and trust that between you, you will be able to mobilise them.

- Think about your abilities and gifts and put down your strengths in relation to what you are trying to achieve with a group. What have you got to bring to the group?

- Ask yourself what you would say to someone who came to you for help or advice on how to cope with their feelings of nervousness or inadequacy.

- Tell yourself that in all probability the group will be better off *with* you than without you! (Being told this early on in my career proved a watershed for me.)

- Ask yourself "what is the worst that can happen?" and then decide what you could do about it.

- Prepare for the meeting carefully so you feel confident and relaxed about the introduction and the methods you will use.

- Remind yourself that other members may also be feeling nervous and be in need of care, attention and encouragement.

- Relax, breathe deeply and try to give an impression of confidence and eagerness as you start: the very posture of your body and your facial expression helps your feelings and helps other people to warm to you.

When feeling negative towards a group or individual members

Experiencing fluctuation of our feelings towards other people, even those nearest and dearest to us, is part of our human condition, a painful part.

- Try using the journalling method suggested by Ira Progoff[4] in relation to any individual or group to whom you feel negative or who inhibits you in some way. Take a few minutes to think about them in a relaxed way, try standing in their shoes and seeing life as they see it. Then on paper start a conversation with them rather as though you are writing a play. Do not think too deeply about what to say, just let the conversation flow. When it dries up, read what you have written, this may set you off again. Try to bring the conversation to some sort of conclusion. After a while reflect on what you have written and see what your feelings now are. The conversation may be opened up again at a later stage.

- Go out of your way to make an overtly friendly gesture towards the group or individuals to whom you feel negative. The idea underlying this, is that acting contrary to your feelings, will help bring them into line with your action.

- Try to think about the good points of the group. Ask yourself how *they* would explain the things which make you feel negative about them.

When you are emotionally involved in an issue

You may find yourself about to work with a group on an issue about which you have strong feelings in favour of or opposed to a certain outcome. In order to remain non-directive and to make your own contribution to the discussion, without putting undue pressure on the group, it may help beforehand to:

- face the fact that your emotional involvement with the issue may distort your objectivity or allow you to coax the discussion in the direction in which you want it to go. This realisation in itself is likely to help you avoid this pitfall;

- look as objectively as you can at all the possible outcomes and the pros and cons of each;

- realise that other people are likely to come with their own emotional response to the issue and decide how to help everyone to be objective. Engendering objectivity is considered in more detail on page 97.

When you fear the unexpected

The unexpected may never happen but fear of it can be inhibiting and, by definition, one cannot prepare for it. You can, however, reduce the range of the unexpected by:

- thinking ahead, envisaging the people with whom you will be working, their possible feelings, thoughts, questions and reactions. Some of the ideas put forward on page 39 may help you in doing this;

- asking yourself: what are the things which often catch me on the hop or worry me? When am I usually beset by sudden requests or questions?

- examining how you have responded to the unexpected in the past, so you can learn what worked or did not work;

- looking through the suggestions of ways in which you could respond to unexpected questions or requests (p. 115) and unhelpful comments (p. 184).

The clearer you are about your purpose and the more habitually you use it in preparing and planning your work, the more likely it is that your spontaneous response to something unexpected will have a positive outcome.

A BRIEF EXERCISE IN RELATION TO NEGATIVE FEELINGS

Work through the following four questions:

(a) What do I find most difficult when coping with emotions of . . . or towards . . . or aroused by . . . ?

(b) What are the feelings this arouses in me?

(c) What would help me to control my emotions and use them positively?

(d) What can I learn from this? An example on such an exercise is given on page 128.

---

4. **Clarifying the authority and responsibility of the group in decision-making**

The group worker and the members need to be clear and agreed about the extent and limits of their authority and power in relation to any involvement they may have in decision-making. It is important to clarify whether:

- the group itself will make the decision, for example, a group responsible for deciding on the subject and speaker for some event;

- the group is being asked for its views and recommendations in the light of which some other person or group will make a decision, for example, a sub-committee of a parish council or management board;

- the group is purely fact-finding, for example, a working party with the task of gathering and sorting out information on a range of options preparatory to their exploration by a decision-making group or assembly;

- if the group is responsible for making a decision, is it also responsible for its implementation; for example, a local voluntary branch of a charity deciding on a fund-raising event?

- the group is accountable for its decisions to another person or body; for example, the executive committee of a trustees' meeting or a chief executive and his seniors responsible to a county council;

- the group is preparing to negotiate by clarifying the various stances it could adopt in response to the demands and needs of other groups; for example, as one of several groups wanting to share the use of premises;

- the main function of a group is to enable its members to help each other learn more about a subject with no remit to make decisions beyond those affecting its own members nor to make recommendations to anyone else although it may decide to do so; for example, a group of people responsible for different functions in a department or organisation and who need to keep abreast of the work and developments in which each one is engaged and discuss the implications for the whole team.

Often the various items on the agenda call for a variety of responses: one item will call for advice, another for an exchange of facts, another for a consultative discussion, and yet another for a decision the group may or may not be responsible for implementing.

Clarifying such matters beforehand and ensuring that members are ready to accept the required degree of responsibility, can be crucial to the success of a meeting and prevent much frustration, heartache and misunderstanding.

5. Confidentiality

The group may, on occasion, be constrained by the confidential nature of the subject: ensuring confidentiality may be necessary if people are to enter freely into the discussion. As it is viewed and practised in a variety of ways, clarification as to what 'confidential' means on any particular occasion is needed:

- Does it include *all* that is said at the meeting or only certain aspects of it? Is this to be decided at the start or will the confidential matters be identified at the end of the meeting?

- Who is included within the area of confidentiality? Are there any people absent from the meeting who need to be told about it? How can you ensure they respect the confidential nature of what they are being told?

- Does it mean not repeating anything which has been said *or* not identifying the speaker or the source? Can anything be quoted if made completely anonymous? Does permission to quote need to be sought from the person(s) concerned?

- What about the note-taking and the circulation of a record? Will the confidential matters be included in the record or not? Is it necessary to put 'strictly confidential' both on the record and on the envelope in which it is posted?

- Have you, as facilitator, information which is confidential to you? (p. 88).

(6.) Establishing objectives for your meeting

Beginning to think about and prepare for a meeting can be difficult. A helpful first step is to ascertain and formulate as accurately and concisely as you can what it is you and the group wish to achieve. Doing this gives you a base from which to plan and, by provoking you to think more deeply, makes it more likely that you will concentrate on what is essential and central. It therefore helps you to design or structure your meeting so that everyone is working to the same end. Objectives need to be checked out with the group at the start of the meeting. Your aim through the initial formulation should be to stimulate open and purposeful thinking, rather than to get people to agree to your formulation. Establishing objectives provides a base line when you or the group come to assess how the meeting went. Ensure your objectives are realistic.

In formulating the objective of a meeting it helps to be clear and specific and to use basic English rather than jargon or technical language. It is also useful to differentiate *what* you want to achieve from *how* you will work to achieve it.

The following are examples of objectives worked on with members of the group. Some groups may find this tedious; the clearer you are before presenting your formulation the better.

Example 1. The director of a long-established firm of lawyers newly setting up in a 'big city' was responsible for designing the floor space, with offices, reception area, library, cloakrooms and conference rooms. The director called a meeting of those who would be working in the converted space and put forward as the objective:

> To work out how we can best design the floor space to include the necessary offices, etc.

As this was discussed it was re-formulated as:

To think out what sort of image of the firm should be projected through the interior design of the floor space.

Further discussion followed and a more specific objective arrived at.

To think out ways in which everything clients experience from when they first set foot on the premises, in terms of light, space, shape, colour, texture etc. gives the impression that here is a multi-national firm with a substantial tradition and ethical values, and which is committed to professional excellence.

In working further certain dangers were perceived and people worked out what they wished to avoid. For instance, to avoid such luxury or flamboyance that clients would feel overwhelmed or think consciously or subconsciously "it's going to cost me £500 to sit down".

Example 2. The leader and voluntary staff of a youth club who come together to plan the programme. The leader's first formulation of an objective was:

To plan a varied programme of events for the next six months.

When they probed a bit deeper they re-worded this as:

To plan a programme to meet the varied needs of different members.

A short discussion of what they meant by 'varied needs' led them to a further formulation:

To plan a programme to help members to develop into mature adults through activities which will meet some of their physical, emotional, intellectual and spiritual needs.

This led them to see that participating in the planning would promote the development of the members and be a first step towards achieving the objective, so they added some of the 'hows' by which they would work at this:

- by having informal conversations, and stimulating new and imaginative ideas;
- by having a 'brainstorming' meeting with all club members;
- by forming a programme planning group representative of staff and members;
- by getting the young people to think not only about what they would like to do but why they would like to do it;
- by feeding in possible activities and exploring what the various activities could lead to.

Example 3. A liturgy group is charged with responsibility for making recommendations about the shape and type of liturgy in their church. The group worker began by formulating the objective to read:

> To work out together ways of getting more participation in the liturgy in our church.

This was unsatisfactory: participation is not always a positive value. People can participate out of fear, participate angrily or superficially. A change was made from 'more participation' to 'better participation'. This too was unsatisfactory: the term 'better' was vague and needed defining. What is behind the desire for better participation? It might be possible to get 'better participation' through a system of rewards or bribes! In exploring why better participation was desired the objective was re-worded:

> To work out ways of ensuring that our liturgy is really meeting people's spiritual needs.

Members of a group with this objective might well spend a great deal of time in working out what these spiritual needs were. Reflecting on this the group re-formulated it once more:

> To work out ways of ensuring that liturgical celebrations are of real help in enabling people to live out their Christian beliefs in their everyday lives.

Such an enlargement and precision in the objective may appear laborious and self-evident, but many shelved and unused reports manifest imprecision on task setting, and energetic working groups which start with enthusiasm can end in frustration, disappointment and wasted effort.

CHECK LIST

Some of the questions which may help check out or improve on your formulation are:

- If I/we achieve this, will it make a substantial difference?
- Could this be achieved and yet have a poor outcome?
- Why do I/we want to achieve this, what is underlying it for me/us?
- Is this a method, i.e., a 'how', rather than a 'what'? (p. 166).
- Is the objective stated clearly and specifically?

II. PREPARING YOUR MATERIAL

In preparing the material which is to form the subject matter of the discussion, the group worker needs to consider the nature of the discussion, to get out its constituent parts in a logical order, to formulate incisive and thought-provoking questions, to decide whether or not to use sub-groups, and to work out how to present the topic clearly, using methods which will be effective and stimulate the group to participate. Although for the sake of clarity these various aspects are dealt with separately, they are inter-related and complementary.

As you think through what you are going to do, keep in mind anything about the participants which is relevant.

1. Marshalling your material and structuring your discussion

As group worker aim to order and arrange the material to be discussed so that it:

- aids systematic thought, thus making for progress rather than circularity;
- focuses on core or generic issues;
- helps people to see the parts in relation to the whole, particularly how any aspect in which they are interested fits into the overall context or scheme of things.

The more complex the issue to be discussed the greater the need to prepare by working out a structure which will facilitate the logical progression of ideas. This structure may well change its shape several times: both in the preparation, when it is presented to the members, and once they start discussing. Any structure must be treated as a servant and not a master.

Thinking creatively: A first step towards formulating a structure is to think creatively about the issue or subject to be discussed (p. 191). Various methods may be employed.

- A 'discursive scribble': Take a sheet of paper sideways on and explore the topic, allowing your mind to roam around it at will, jotting down ideas and questions as they occur. This can be done at one sitting or over a few days and is best worked at during one's most creative time of day, whether early morning or late at night.

- Diagrams: Clarifying your mind by putting things down in diagrammatic form is another way of stimulating yourself to think about the various aspects of the subject or situation (p. 66).

- Patterning: A method described by Tony Buzan.[5] This involves writing the topic in the centre of a page and bringing to mind any ideas connected with it. Some ideas may spark off others. Write these down on interconnected lines. Buzan advises writing in capitals for easier reading. Your mind will work faster than your pencil so simply let your writing flow, do not pause to think about where things should go or connect up as that will slow down your creativity. Any necessary tidying up can be done afterwards. Below is an example.

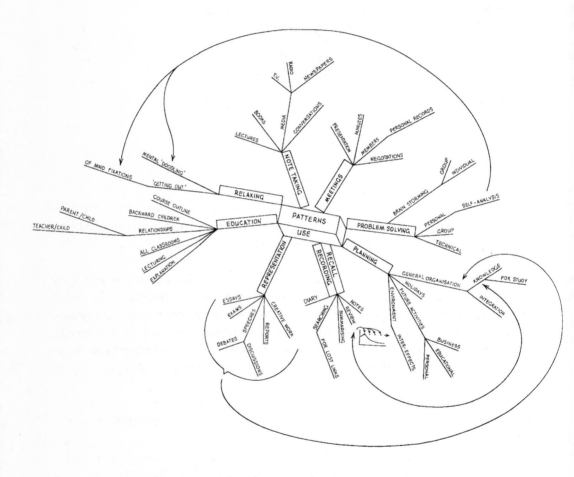

Gabriele Lurser Rico[6] has a similar method which she calls Clustering "a non-linear brainstorming process akin to free association". This stimulates the same sort of free association of ideas using circles.

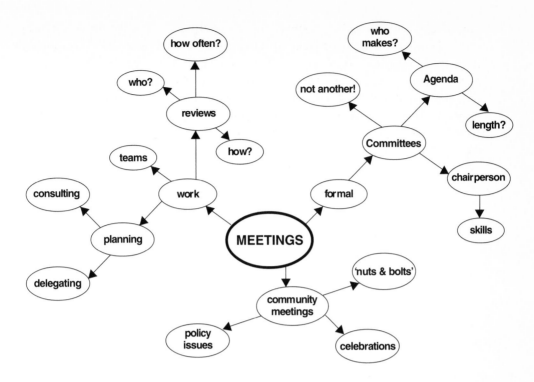

Thorough preliminary thinking by the facilitator is useful when it identifies and clarifies the underlying questions which must be worked at and the order in which they can best be tackled.

Formulating a structure: The next step is to put some shape into the material by sorting it into constituent parts and then ordering the points so they flow constructively one from another. In the process you are likely to become clearer about your ideas and new ones will occur to you. Ask yourself: "What are the key questions which helped me to explore this topic?" Formulating these questions will help you to open up each area of the topic for critical consideration by others (p. 56).

Below is an example of the structure prepared for a discussion on team work.

1. What do we mean by 'team work'?
   What sort of team work do we want to promote? (Clarify and agree.)

2. Whom do we want to promote 'team work' with and why:
   (a) those in authority over us?
   (b) colleagues?
   (c) other organisations?
   (d) clients?
   (Sub-group work on each. Pool and discuss.)

3. What prevents or hinders effective team work?

4. What makes for effective 'team work'? (Pause for thought on 3 and 4 and then brainstorm on each.)

5. Implications: what do we need to do, stop doing, avoid immediately or over a longer term, in relation to the various groups with which we want to promote team work? (Work in sub-groups, pool, discuss and decide. Stress need to be practical and realistic.)

The most appropriate underlying structure will vary with the type of meeting. A decision-making group or a group called to make recommendations to another group, for example, is likely to find it helpful to gather all the facts first, then analyse them and weigh their significance, before making a decision (p. 161 on 'Decision making'). A group facing a difficulty may find the problem-tackling sequence outlined on page 74 useful. Structures such as these help to prevent individual members from rushing forward too soon to present their own preferred solution.

Some groups without decisions to make may well thrive better on a looser structure – indeed structure may emerge as the discussion progresses. At such times, while listening to a discursive discussion, you may be able to see a way of organising the ideas and summarising them so they have shape and coherence. Skill in finding the connections between points being made and putting them into a meaningful pattern is hard to develop but worth every effort. Ways of developing this skill are described on pages 110 and 123.

Ways of testing out and using a structure are described on page 89 'Using and not misusing your preparatory work'.

WHY AM I STUCK?

How often have I sat down to prepare a meeting and found myself up against a brick wall: few ideas emerge; those which do, turn to dust as I contemplate them; every avenue seems blocked, every suggestion arrives heavy footed. This can be a painful time of gestation. What can help? Try one of the following:

- Tell yourself that this happens to many people: writers, scientists and thinkers of all kinds. Remind yourself that it passes. Creativity takes time. Ideas which grow mushroom-wise are not the most long lasting. Remember past experiences and how you came through them.

- Use the problem-tackling sequence described on page 74.
- Ask yourself:

  Why am I stuck?

  What am I trying to do?

  What is concerning me?

  Why can't I think about it?

  What am I trying to say? work out?

  What is important?

  What's preventing me?

  Why can't I work it out?[7]

- Give yourself a break and do some activity which you enjoy and which is likely to re-energise you.

These ideas can also be useful when a group reaches an impasse. This situation is considered on page 113.

2. **The nature of the discussion: general or specific**[8]

Topics and issues may be considered in general terms or studied through a particular incident or situation. These alternatives and what each demands of members are considered below.

A general discussion is one which centres on common problems, issues, or general principles and in which members contribute ideas and insights from their own experience, without recounting in detail the specific examples on which they are drawing.

General discussions occur frequently on training courses and are found useful by people, such as managers or workers wanting to air new ideas; members of residential communities wanting to probe more deeply the ideals on which their life is based; a college staff formulating guidelines for keeping lines of communication open between the different departments; or a group of professional workers wanting to share insights and learn from each other about motivating people to take responsibility for the work of the organisation.

To engage in a general discussion people have to:

- make connections between their experience of specific examples and the general points made. Where people cannot see a connection it is helpful to explore with them why this is so;
- make points succinctly, avoiding lengthy anecdotes which could turn it into a discussion of a specific case;
- apply what is learnt in general terms to their specific experience and situation and be able to assess whether or not it is relevant and appropriate.

A specific discussion studies a particular instance or situation and draws from it general conclusions which members can apply to their own situations. For example, rather than having a general discussion on how to establish and keep to priorities in one's work, a group could specifically discuss how Jack can do so in his situation.

To engage in a specific discussion people have to:

- be prepared to concentrate on understanding the case or example until they have really grasped it;
- recall their own experience and extract and use ideas and insights from it to raise questions or make points in relation to the incident being discussed, without allowing their own situation or experience to obtrude. A 'no anecdotes' rule can be helpful;
- relate whatever comes out of the discussion by way of general principles to their specific situation or experience.

A specific, rather than a general discussion, is more likely to be needed by a group meeting to solve a particular problem it is up against, to make a decision, or to plan a course of action.

Case studies are examples of specific discussion. T.R. Batten has developed a structured method of working on case studies which are examples of specific discussion. This is described on page 129.

Differentiating between general and specific discussion clarifies their appropriate uses, alerts a group worker to the difficulties which can emerge from drifting inadvertently from one to the other, and enables you to give clear instructions or suggestions to the group and so avoid misunderstanding and confusion.

3. **A 'concluding check list'** (p. 119)

As you prepare for a meeting it can be helpful to jot down a check list of points you need to raise before the meeting ends. These may concern practical matters or be to do with the subject matter of the meeting or of past or future meetings. A co-worker can perform a useful function in reminding you towards the end of the meeting of anything not covered.

4. **Introduction to questions and questioning**

Reflecting on one's own varied responses to other people's questions reveals the importance of the art of questioning. Formulating and asking questions is one of the principal skills of the facilitator who aims to promote a discussion in which people freely participate and in which they think creatively about a task or a topic. All questions need to take these two aspects into account, the emphasis depending on the objective of the meeting. Participation could be more important if the objective is to enable people to exchange thoughts and feelings in order to build up the sense of community. Thinking creatively could be more important if the task is to make a decision with far-reaching implications.

There are six areas of questioning which need to be considered by a facilitator in relation to the questions which emerge as you think about a topic and begin to structure a discussion.

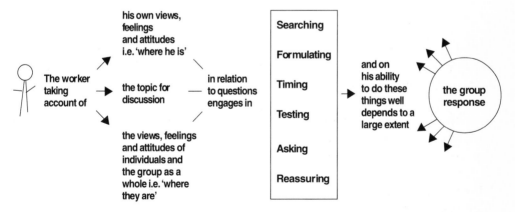

Searching:
is about finding questions which not only stimulate people to think deeply and critically about what is central to the topic in hand but which motivate them to do so.

Formulating:	is about wording the question clearly in basic English, avoiding jargon and technical or emotive language (p. 109).
Timing:	is both about when to ask certain questions, waiting for the best moment to do so, and making opportunities for people to collect their thoughts before responding.
Testing:	is about checking out that the question is acceptable to the group and its exploration is likely to be productive.
Asking:	is about one's manner: putting questions in a sympathetic, understanding and non-threatening manner, which encourages people to share their thoughts and feelings.
Reassuring:	is about putting questions in such a way that people know their responses will be listened to and taken into account.

Although some thought needs to be given to each area, both before and during a meeting, the following points are especially relevant during your preparation.

Searching questions: Questions need to be searching, open and relevant. Aim for a question which is thought provoking and stimulates an honest exchange of ideas and feelings, which goes to the heart of issues of real concern, and is seen to be relevant to the task or topic. If your questions are sequential, the discussion is more likely to flow logically. If they are earthed appropriately in experience and reality, they are likely to be productive. For instance, in a discussion with a group of people coming up to retirement, the facilitator drew on their experience by asking them to reflect on their life at work, at home and on holiday and identify the key activities which they had found most rewarding, stimulating and enjoyable over the last ten years. They were then asked to think of one or two activities which attracted them but which they had either not had time for or never tried. They were then asked what they each hoped for or expected from their retirement. From this the facilitator went on to clarify what they saw retirement to be about, that is, its purpose, which needs to be central to any discussion on the subject.

Some questions may be asked to elicit factual information, others to facilitate the analysis of that information or to find out what people think and feel about it, others again may be to stretch people's minds to think more deeply or creatively exploring new ground together. Some of the simplest questions can be among the most helpful. Rudyard Kipling writes:

I had six serving men
they taught me all I know,
their names were **what** and **why** and **when**
and **where** and **how** and **who**.[9]

I try to search for questions which will make me and others think about things in a new way. It takes time and effort to discover useful questions. You may find the following questions help you in your search:

(a) What are the questions I need to ask myself in order to explore this subject? It stimulates me to have a personal brainstorming session when I write down every question I can think of.

(b) Which of these questions gets to the central issue? Take a critical look at the questions, possibly classify them and pick out the most penetrating.

(c) What is the best order in which to ask them?

(d) What do I need to say by way of introduction?

Formulating questions: Having found searching questions the next task is to word them in a way which the particular group will warm to and clearly understand. To aid this process I use words which are:

– in their common currency rather than mine;

– expressed accurately, clearly and unambiguously;

– non-emotive: rousing emotions can cloud clear thinking. Words and the wording of questions can engender strong positive or negative feelings of anger, fear, unrealistic hopes, etc., all of which can promote too little, inappropriate, or unhelpful participation (p. 109);

– likely to encourage the type of discussion envisaged (Is it to be formal or informal, factual, analytical, practical or theoretical? Is it to provide an exchange of thoughts only or of thoughts and feelings?);

– unbiased. My views or prejudices could lead me to ask a loaded question (p. 38).

For instance, rather than ask a direct and rather hard question such as: "Why do you do such and such?", a more acceptable softer approach would be to re-phrase it: "Can you help me to see why you do x? What does it mean to you?" or "I'm not sure I fully understand what is behind this for you and what you think and feel about it?"

Timing your questions: The first question is likely either to motivate people and reassure them that the time spent is likely to be interesting, *or* to put them off in some way. Ideally the first question is one which everyone is able and willing to think about and contribute to. A question which draws on their experience and is not too demanding may well be a good starter. Once a group has got going it is possible to move with safety to more difficult searching questions.

Testing questions: A range of early questions can ensure that the subject matter, question, or task is something people are motivated to work at because they see it as relevant and useful. It may well be necessary, first of all, to provide background information, summarise the situation or explain the context and suggest where it could lead in terms of further questions, insights, decisions or conclusions. Questions to test the acceptability of the topic are important if people are to enter into the discussion with commitment (p. 37). Such questions need not only be about the content of the meeting but about the way in which you suggest it could be tackled.

According to the topic, testing for acceptability can be more or less stringent by asking: "Do you think working at this question will help us to grapple with...? Is this relevant or likely to be productive?" or "Are you prepared to have a go at this?" The questions asked to test these things out must be put in such a way that people not only think seriously about them but feel free to say what they feel and think without losing face. For instance, "Do you respond positively or negatively to this? Is anyone uneasy?" It is more helpful to say: "Have I made this clear? Is this clear? Does this make sense?" than: "Are you clear? Do you understand?" At times, it could be necessary to allow people time to discuss with their neighbour whether or not the task or question is likely to prove useful.

It takes time to consider and agree whether and how to tackle a topic or task but in the long run it can save time and avoid frustration and wasted energy.

Asking questions and *reassuring as you question* are considered on pages 93 and 94.

A CHECK LIST OF QUESTIONS

This check list is primarily written for use before a meeting when you are preparing your questions and thinking about questioning. However, it can also be adapted for use afterwards by way of evaluation. Using it is a way of increasing your questioning skills. A useful exercise to test out the suitability of your questions is to stand in the shoes of group members and imagine how you would react to them (p. 74).

Searching: Is this question likely to raise issues of real concern and get to the heart of things? Will this question make people think? Have I avoided questions which only lead to 'Yes' or 'No'? Would I find myself able and stimulated to have a go at this question were I a member of this group?

Formulating: Are my questions accurate, clear, unambiguous with the parts properly separated? It can confuse people to ask an "Is it this or that" type of question. Have I avoided unhelpful jargon and technical terms? Is it likely to make them respond objectively, critically, openly or defensively?

Timing: Does my first question give an easy lead into the discussion? Do I need to make a pause and allow people time to think? Do people need prior warning of any question?

Testing: Could this question be put in different ways, repeated in different words, so that it really communicates to people? How can I ensure people think about whether the question is a potentially useful one to work at before starting to answer it? Could I test out my questions on a colleague or friend or someone who knows those concerned or is one of them?

QUESTIONING: *An example from a Team Ministry Meeting*

Some questions from a meeting of a team of vicars illustrate the use of these six aspects of questioning, and show how each can be used at the appropriate time and often in combination.

The team rector responsible for coordinating the activities of the team, knew that feelings of mistrust and even resentment towards himself and to each other existed within the team and he felt this underlying disharmony was affecting their work as a team. Yet on the surface they were kind to each other and to him, behaving in a way that, as Christians, they expected themselves to behave.

The rector decided that he would attempt to help the team to a deeper understanding of their respective roles by encouraging an open expression of their honest feelings.

At the next weekly meeting, after the routine administration had been settled he asked, "Today can we spend a little time discussing how we all view my role as team coordinator and the relationship of all our roles to each other and how we can best use these meetings to help our work? I have had time to think about my role, so you may like a few minutes to reflect and perhaps jot down some thoughts."

This opening was:
  Searching and directly related to his objective.
  Formulated in simple language.
  Asked in a sympathetic and non-threatening manner.

In particular the issue of interpersonal relationships was depersonalized by referring to the relationship between roles – not to the people fulfilling them.

The *Timing* was correct, the routine administration had been done and team members were offered time to collect their thoughts and feelings.

They were *reassured* that all these contributions would be listened to, by him and hopefully, by each other. *Testing* was not done at the start but when the vicar gained a defensive response from one member who said, "I think we are working very well together as a team." The rector tested the general feeling by building on this opening, he asked in a reassuring way "Well that's good to hear, so it might help to look at the ways in which we work well together and then maybe consider areas where we can still hope to improve." Looking first at the positive side, builds people's confidence to face the negative facts.

III. DECIDING HOW TO WORK

1. Alone or with a colleague?

My experience is that the more complex the task of the meeting, the greater need I have to enlist the help of a colleague to be my co-worker in order to help me prepare for the meeting, help and support me during it, and learn from it afterwards. Using a co-worker is also a way of inducting a person into these approaches (p. 189). I often exchange roles with a co-worker.

A colleague needs to be someone you can trust, who will be supportive and encouraging while at the same time bringing a critical and creative mind to bear on the content of the meeting, and be perceptive and sensitive in relation to the members.

The following describes some functions of a co-worker showing the possibilities of this role.

Beforehand: Your co-worker can prepare with you from scratch or can check through your preparation, considering what you are aiming to do, how you are planning to do it, the likely or possible reaction of the participants, and any problems you foresee.

During the meeting: The co-worker, as appropriate, could support you, encourage the members, mediate between them, clarify points, move the discussion on, and be time keeper. This is described in greater detail on page 95.

After the meeting: A discussion between you and your co-worker, from your different perspectives, can enable you both to learn from the experience, and highlight any action which needs to be taken by way of follow-up (p. 131).

2. The use of sub-groups

As groups increase in size the opportunity for everyone to participate diminishes and it can therefore be useful to divide members into small groups for part of a meeting. This may be planned beforehand or be spontaneous. A sub-group may be as small as two or three people or far larger depending on the size of the total group. Even in groups as small as six it can sometimes be useful to divide people into pairs. Sub-groups may meet in different rooms or be together in the same room. Three or more groups in a room are better than two: with only two groups they tend to hear and distract each other. Here we consider the potential value of using sub-groups, ways in which they can be formed, and different methods by which they can present their findings. All this needs to be thought about before a meeting. Introducing and working with sub-groups during a meeting will be found on page 101.

The value of sub-groups

The use of sub-groups during a discussion:

- increases participation as it allows more people to talk at once;
- changes the pace and atmosphere and provides variety. When people are tense, somnolent or apathetic, sub-groups provide an opportunity to help them engage in the discussion in a different setting. For instance, it was found that forming members of an industrial work force into small working teams had a beneficial effect on their morale, interest in the task and output;[10]
- helps the shy or more reticent people to make their contribution (p. 135) and limits the dominance of the more vocal (p. 138): allows for more intimate exchanges between people;
- is a way of getting a lot of different ideas and opinions voiced, or more complex and difficult issues explored at greater depth;
- can defuse potentially destructive discussion of emotive issues by providing an opportunity for all views to be articulated and listened to with understanding in the small group, and to be reported to the larger group so that they are more likely to be considered objectively;
- provides you as facilitator with a break in which you can clarify your ideas, prepare a summary of what has emerged so far or confer with your co-worker.

Forming sub-groups

If you are going to use sub-groups, you are faced with choosing whether to form them in an *ad hoc* way, determine the size and membership yourself, or allow members to select their own group. This choice may well affect the value of the outcome. However they are formed you need to ensure the members are willing to work in them (p. 101).

Ad hoc groups: Chance or *ad hoc* groups can be formed by suggesting people talk to their immediate neighbours (buzz groups), by numbering off or by using some other random method of selection. People are probably sitting next to their friends: different *ad hoc* methods are likely either to keep friends together or to mix them up. Which is most appropriate?

Self-selection: There are disadvantages of simply inviting people to form themselves into groups: it can cause embarrassment as people tend to gravitate to those they know, and some people may get left out and find it hurtful or worrying. However, it can be useful to invite people to select the group according to the topic to be discussed: put the subject headings on sheets of paper and ask people to sign up according to their preference. Sometimes the size of the sub-group is of little consequence so long as there is a minimum number to do the task, but if you want groups of equal size indicate this on each sheet: as soon as one group is complete, people have to sign up on another, or negotiate with someone willing to move to another group.

Determining membership: If you decide to form the groups beforehand bear in mind such things as existing relationships, work situations, views, disciplines, qualifications, skills, perceptions, sensitivity, quality of mind and heart, etc. If you do not know people well enough to make informed decisions you could seek the assistance of someone who does.

In working with a group over a period of time, there are advantages of keeping to the same sub-groups as people get to know and trust each other and find a way of working well together. However, you need to be aware that some people may not be happy in their group or the group itself may not function satisfactorily. One advantage of varying the sub-groups for different sessions is that everyone has a chance to work with everyone else, but remember that a newly formed sub-group takes extra time to settle down to work.

Types of sub-groups

According to the purpose of a particular meeting you may want *heterogeneous* or *homogeneous* groups.

Heterogeneous groups: It can be useful to have heterogeneous groups which highlight the differences between people if you want:

– members of different disciplines to contribute their expertise to a common task;

– to help people who are very different from one another to know, understand and appreciate each other and different points of view;

– people who are likely to be implicated in different ways to think through policy decisions which will affect their lives, work and future. This gives them an opportunity to consider the effects of different options on different people. For example, mixed groups could help management and workers of a small firm consider the implications of expansion in relation to finances, staffing and accommodation and understand and appreciate the very different views emerging;

– people to come to a common view of their work or articulate a common purpose. For example, members of an organisation wanting to formulate a mission statement, or a religious community discussing greater involvement with minorities, or youth workers in a locality determining future emphases, could find it easier to hammer out their differences and begin to work towards unanimity.

Examples of heterogeneous groups

Snowball: members work in pairs for a limited time and then two pairs join to form a foursome, two foursomes to form a group of eight, and so on. Give instructions to get out key points or common ideas each time the group is reformed.

Pyramid:[11] this is similar to the above as members move from pairs to larger numbers. As each stage introduce a higher level of generality so that at each stage new ground is always being tackled. This makes it possible to make a transfer from, say personal experience, to the general and then the conceptual.

Homogeneous groups: However, homogeneous groups can be helpful if you want people unused to sharing their deeper thoughts and feelings to do so. It may help to start putting people with similar views and feelings together so they express their fears and hopes in a supportive atmosphere and later mix people up so they hear other people's very different ideas and views.

Alternatively if you want groups to work on a number of different tasks, form each group according to those best able to do the particular task.

Reporting back

This needs to be thought about beforehand so that groups can be briefed adequately. In deciding how sub-groups should report back it is useful to consider the objective of the meeting, the size of the group, the time available, and what is known or likely to be acceptable to the participants. Below are some ways in which findings can be shared.

- Ask a member of each group to meet afterwards, possibly with you: together make a summary of the points to be reported verbally and/or in writing. This is a useful method for large conferences where listening to a plethora of reports can dull one's receptivity.

- Ask each group to put its report on a large sheet of paper. This encourages people to be specific and succinct.

- Ask for a verbal report. You may need to ask for the written notes to be handed in afterwards. To prevent repetition (although at times this can be useful) you can suggest that each speaker add only what has not been mentioned already. This may call for skills not possessed by many reporters.

- Suggest groups are 'creative' in their reporting back, using drama, symbols, art, etc: this can take time and is therefore more suitable for longer courses or conferences.

- 'Snowball or pyramid' (p. 64): Instruct people to get out the key points or common ideas each time the group is re-formed.

- Tell members that feedback will be optional *or* that there will be no direct reporting of what has been discussed. This is suitable for more personal and intimate sharing. At times it is useful afterwards to ask a question which either takes the subject on a stage or is about what members thought or felt about the exercise.

Ways of handling the reports are discussed on page 103.

CHECK LIST TO HELP YOU DECIDE
ON THE USE OF SUB-GROUPS

Will I use sub-groups:
  – to help people relax at the start?
  – to encourage quieter people to participate?
  – to limit the dominance of an individual?
  – to stimulate more creative thinking?
  – to get out a variety of ideas?
  – to make sharing in depth easier?
  – to allow people to express pent-up feelings?
  – to save time?

Is there any danger of people not wanting to work in groups? (p. 101).

How shall I form them: *ad hoc*? through self-selection? or plan them
myself?
Would mixed or homogenous groups be most effective?
What criteria should I use to select them?
What about existing relationships: is anyone likely to inhibit anyone
else?
Who gets on well together?
Who thinks creatively? openly/critically? undefensively?
What size would be best?
Where should they meet?
What sort of report would be appropriate?

3. Methods and their presentation

Using different methods can motivate people to enter into the meeting and
stimulate them to think (p. 91). The methods used and the way they are presented need to take into account both what will be appropriate and effective
in terms of the task or topic, and what is likely to be acceptable, attractive and
helpful to the team or group. Sometimes simplicity and clarity are called for,
at others something more imaginative and elaborate. Some occasions demand
customary and routine procedures, others variety and innovation.

Various methods are briefly outlined below with the aim of giving sufficient
information about their use to allow an informed choice to be made. Many of
the more imaginative methods are best suited to community groups, conferences, training courses and study groups rather than to project or work teams.
Beware of using a method simply as a gimmick.

*Diagrams, charts and symbols** (p. 98)

As human beings we have an amazing ability to receive and make sense of
information from our environment. In everyday life we rely on far more than
words as we interpret traffic lights and road signs, architects' drawings and
maps, clock faces and advertisements. Although words may be used to com-
plement or supplement them, these things do not rely solely on words to indicate their meaning.

---

* For the purpose of this book these terms refer to any visual representations, be they pictorial
or abstract.

Diagrams, charts and symbols draw on a wide repertoire of mental skills. Some people prefer the more imaginative, spacial, illustrative and holistic to the verbal, analytic or sequential mode of operating. On the whole this side of our minds is less developed. Research on the brain provides some interesting insights into the value of diagrams and models.[12] Their use calls for imagination and creative skills on the part of the facilitator.

In this section I limit myself to outlining ways in which I have found them useful and factors to be taken into account in deciding whether or not to use them and how to do so. Below are some of the chief uses for which I have used diagrams, charts or symbols:

- To clarify an issue or problem when introducing it or as it is discussed, for example, discussing a situation of faction.

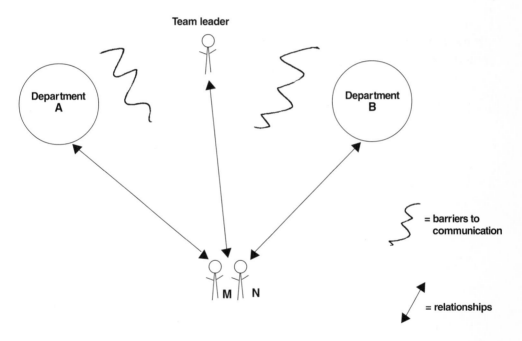

Only two people, M and N are in good relationship with both departments and with the team leader who is isolated. This raises questions about what the team leader can do with M and N to create better relationships all round. Such things may not be seen until the constituent parts are separated in this way. Depicting the situation like this is often called 'a disclosure model' because it reveals something of the underlying dynamics or inner structure and shows connections in such a way as to give insight into what is happening, in order to decide what to do in a situation.[13]

- To explain or explore how the various parts of an organisation fit together. The diagram below shows the relationship and lack of it between the chairperson and the various sub-committees.

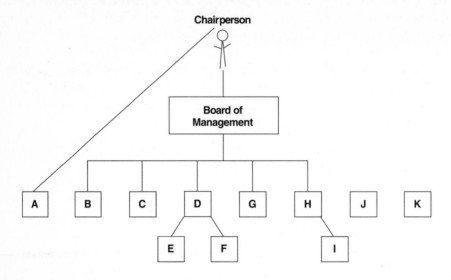

This diagram immediately raises questions and possible dangers. For instance, sub-committee A by-passes the Board of Management and J and K do not report back to anyone.

- To present the current situation in a group or organisation in the light of past history and the context in which it operates, in order to raise questions about its future direction, for example, with a voluntary agency or religious order.

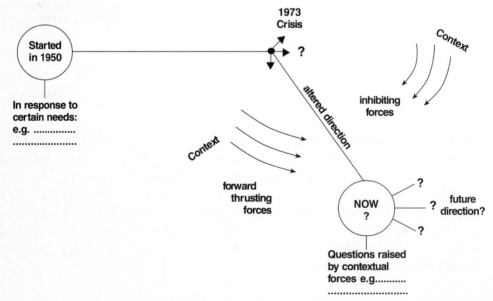

- To clarify for people the situation they are in, for example, with personnel returning home to the UK after years of service overseas.[14]

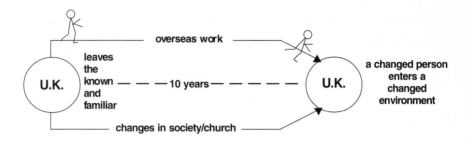

- Planning: clarifying what needs to be done and in what order, by whom and by when, for example, in setting up a conference:

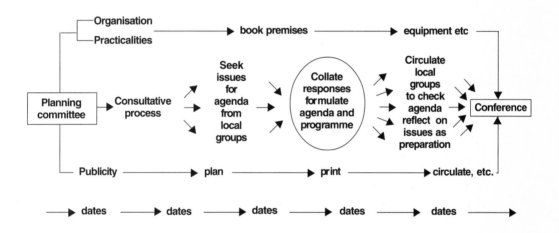

- To compare different models or situations or ways of doing things, for example, in terms of leadership.

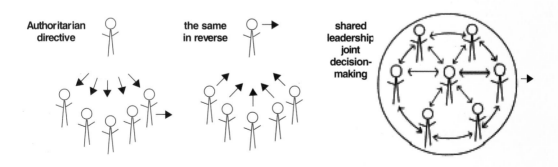

A group could model their past and present practice and decide on the basis of the pros and cons of each model what their preferred practice will be in future. For a fuller treatment see page 186-187.

- To create an appropriate atmosphere for the task in hand. For instance, in a session in which people will be asked to reflect deeply, music, flowers, colour, or art may help.[15]

- To help people get in touch with their feelings. For this the use of symbols can be particularly effective (p. 109). For instance, working with members of an organisation struggling to come to terms with the necessity for radical change, I asked them to relax, to reflect on the organisation and to see what symbol arose in their mind's eye. Paper and felt pens were provided for those who wished. After some minutes people shared in pairs and then in the whole group. This enabled people to voice their fears and pain in a vivid and powerful way in a supportive atmosphere.

- To summarise a discussion (p. 110).

Developing your skills: A good way of developing an ability to use diagrams and charts is to try things out on your own, for instance, to clarify the situation or topic when preparing for a meeting or to make a visual summary of a discussion. The following steps were worked out by Lovell:[16]

i. Get out the key factors:

    What strikes me as I consider this situation or topic or as I listen to what is being said? What stands out for me?

    What do I want to show or illustrate through this diagram?

    What are the principal entities?

ii. Search for connections between them: how do they fit or not fit together?

    What is the interaction between them? How do I picture them in relation to one another? How do they connect/not connect? How can I picture the interaction between the different parts by using arrows, dotted or continuous lines, etc.?

iii. Have I omitted anything? What about the context?

iv. Search for a way of portraying this on paper. Feel free to try all sorts of different ways until one seems to be more accurate or to speak to you.

Deciding on their use: During your preparation you need to consider whether or not you will use diagrams, charts or symbols, and if so what kind, when and how. For instance, a group may be small enough to sit more informally round a sheet of paper on a table rather than face a flip chart. You may do a diagram and bring it ready made or draw it as you talk to it. Many people who discount 'finished' diagrams in books will find those built up in front of them useful. Visual representations are often particularly effective with less literate groups. You may produce a diagram or ask the members to do so. Making these choices is an integral part of your preparation for a meeting. Introducing the use of diagrams is discussed on page 98.

Work-sheets

Work-sheets are questionnaires consisting of a few questions with space for people to jot down their replies: these may be used as a basis for discussion in a group or for member's private use beforehand. Work-sheets can be particularly useful in small groups working without a designated leader. They help people keep to the point and work systematically, knowing the amount of ground they are expected to cover.

Work-sheets need clear instructions and unambiguous questions. Number the questions and ask groups to work through them sequentially or ask different groups to start with different questions, so that each question is covered by at least one group.

Imagination can be used in their presentation, with one or more sheets of paper folded in various ways. I often fold an A4 sheet, write a brief introduction and have one or two questions on the front. The inside pages may be used vertically and/or horizontally or divided into columns. Using the space creatively can be a motivating factor and encourage people in their use.

'Table-cloth discussion'

This maximises participation and uses the resources of the members to get out the aspects of a subject which people want to work on, or to form an agenda. This is best done in a group small enough to sit round a table on which is a large sheet of paper with the topic written in the centre. Go through the steps below asking people:

– to use their bit of the 'table-cloth' to write down the aspects they want to discuss. In a discussion on retirement people wrote such questions as: When do I begin to prepare for it? How am I going to use my time? What is retirement for? Dangers and pitfalls? Hopes and opportunities?

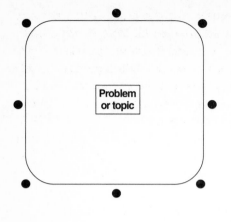

- to number their points in the order in which they could best be tackled.

- to read out their first question so you can decide together where to begin.

Discuss all number one questions before going on to people's second and subsequent questions. As you proceed pick up any related questions which happen to be in different places on people's lists. You or a member of the group can use the space on the 'table-cloth' to jot down or summarise key points.

Should you be working with more than one table of people, you could write the instructions on 'table napkins' placed face down with the number on the reverse, so the group can work its own way through the steps.

Role play and imagination

In this section I describe the use of various activities: a prepared playlet, role play, 'fantasy journeys', and standing in someone else's shoes.

The prepared playlet. This is the acting out of a script which illustrates some issue or problem to serve as a basis for discussion.[17]

Role play.[18] This term covers a wide variety of activities and is used to stimulate or tease out a problem.

In one form, a number of people are asked to take certain roles and spontaneously act out an imagined situation, say, a committee, community meeting, or an event. People then discuss how they experienced the role play and what they learnt from it. This type of role play is often used on human development training courses.

Another way of using role play is to involve all members of the group in working out an issue. For example, working with a group of people recently returned to the UK after spending a long period of service overseas, one of the questions they posed was: "Is now the best time to make major decisions about a change of direction in one's life or work?" I divided them into three groups. Group A were to seek advice on the question, Group B thought now *was* the right time, and Group C thought now *was not* the right time. The A's, B's and

C's were given five minutes in their groups to prepare: the A's pictured their situations and prepared their questions, the B's and C's marshalled their arguments. The role play itself took ten minutes in groups of three made up of one member from each of Groups A, B and C. A asked the questions and responded to the views of B and C. The results were pooled and discussed.

Role play can also be used in case studies (p. 129) when, after discussion, members still disagree or are uncertain as to whether a particular approach would achieve the desired result. Two or three members are asked to act it out, this is discussed, improvements suggested and re-enacted until it becomes clear what is most likely to work in such a situation.[19]

There are some golden rules which can be usefully adopted in all forms of role play:

- Avoid casting vulnerable or timid people with roles in which their weak spots will be shown up.

- De-brief people after the sketch: uncomplimentary labels can get stuck on people with damaging results.[20]

- Stop the role play when its aim has been achieved and people have sufficient information or empathise with it. The discussion which follows is valuable in teasing out the insights and understandings which have been gained. Occasionally it can be useful to re-play the scene trying another tack.

If everyone is not taking part it may be useful to engage the audience by getting each individual or sub-group to identify themselves with a specific character, particularly one who has an opposing viewpoint to their own. Or they can be asked to look at particular issues, questions, behaviour, etc.

A fantasy journey. This is an imaginative tour guided by the facilitator, at a slow pace, to allow members to experience the journey in their thoughts and their feelings. Members are asked to close their eyes and sit in a relaxed and comfortable position. A quiet and reflective atmosphere can be induced by soft music, dim lights or a visual aid, such as flowers, a picture of a 'still life', or a symbol such as a rock, piece of quartz or a candle.

Members are asked to go back to some experience in their life, such as when they moved house, returned from overseas, joined a community or organisation, started a new job, had a moment of insight or 'conversion', and to relive it. Or, they could be asked to imagine themselves in a situation in order to empathise with it, for example, a paraplegic in a wheelchair so they feel some of their everyday frustrations and fears. Fantasy journeys can be conducted into a story or incident with individuals being asked to identify with one of the characters.[21]

Although many people are able to enter into this kind of experience, some people find it hard or are unable to do so and may react negatively to the idea. The use of fantasy is so potentially valuable in one's life, it is worth giving some thought as to how to encourage such people to try it out.

Standing in another's shoes: An ability to do this increases one's sensitivity to other people and can be seen as part of, or prior to, group discussion. It can be particularly useful to get people to stand in the shoes of those whose views and experience is very different from their own.

A problem-tackling sequence[22]

This sequence of steps in tackling a problem is discussed here because the facilitator may find it provides a structure for the discussion which can be used overtly with a group.

By way of preamble, it is important to realise that difficulties and problems are everyday occurrences, they are to be tackled rather than to be possessed or bemoaned. A change of orientation comes from talking about 'facing a problem' rather than 'having a problem'.[23] This also gets away from thinking of oneself or other people as 'problems'. It can also be encouraging to realise that the higher your purposes and the harder the thing you are trying to do, the greater the difficulties and problems you face. Climbing Everest is more fraught with potential hazards than climbing Snowdon.

People will be motivated to work at a problem if they feel there is some chance of making progress towards its solution or amelioration. If people are uncertain or reluctant it may help to negotiate a time limit: "Can we give an hour to it and see if we can get somewhere?"

The notes below refer to the steps on the chart opposite.

Step 1: *What is the Problem?* Clarification of the difficulty and of the terms used can help to ensure not only that people are talking about the same thing but that the *real* difficulty is discussed. When a team leader sought my help, he said, "The problem is Mr White who dominates our discussion." A few questions elicited the clarification that the real problem was that other team members were not contributing their

PROBLEM TACKLING SEQUENCE

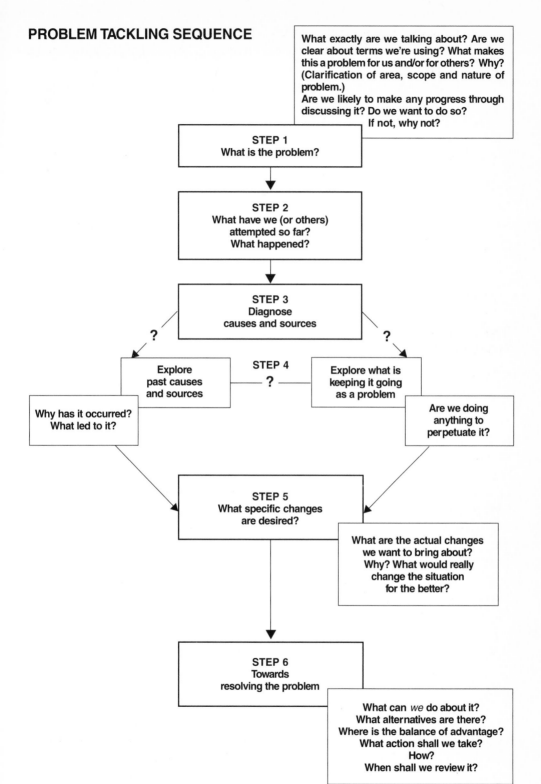

What exactly are we talking about? Are we clear about terms we're using? What makes this a problem for us and/or for others? Why? (Clarification of area, scope and nature of problem.)
Are we likely to make any progress through discussing it? Do we want to do so?
If not, why not?

STEP 1
What is the problem?

STEP 2
What have we (or others) attempted so far?
What happened?

STEP 3
Diagnose causes and sources

?   ?

Explore past causes and sources

STEP 4
?

Explore what is keeping it going as a problem

Why has it occurred?
What led to it?

Are we doing anything to perpetuate it?

STEP 5
What specific changes are desired?

What are the actual changes we want to bring about? Why? What would really change the situation for the better?

STEP 6
Towards resolving the problem

What can *we* do about it?
What alternatives are there?
Where is the balance of advantage?
What action shall we take?
How?
When shall we review it?

ideas and insights because Mr White contributed so many, took up so much time, and generally sapped the energy of the group. This re-formulation widened the problem and led people to consider not only Mr White's participation but that of the other group members.

Step 2: *What have we (or others) attempted so far?* Investigating what people have already done and what happened as a result, can throw additional light on the difficulty, and lessen the likelihood of people becoming defensive or exasperated as suggestion after suggestion is turned down because "it didn't work when we tried before."

Step 3: *Diagnosis of causes and sources of the problem.* At this point there is a difficult choice between exploring the initial causes and sources of the problem or focusing on those which are currently keeping it going. Reviewing the history of a problem may be necessary if it helps people to understand it and points towards what can be done about it. However, it can also prove demoralising and paralysing: the rehearsal of old arguments can fuel the problem and re-activate painful emotions; the complex factors and analyses may be more than we can handle and may even inhibit fresh thinking and distract from searching for a way forward. On the other hand, the discovery of what is keeping the problem alive is likely to provide clues for future action.

Step 4: *What specific changes are desired and why?* It can be difficult but rewarding to try to identify in specific terms the key change which would really improve the situation. Again it will be a pointer for future action.

Step 5: *Towards resolving the problem.* It is only useful to discuss a problem from the point of view of what one can do about it *oneself*. It is no good deciding the problem would be solved if X did such and such unless we can see our way to approach X on the matter. Use imagination and lateral thinking[24] to get out all the options and explore each one in turn. Considering the pros and cons and possible effects will increase objectivity and therefore the likelihood of agreeing on a way forward which is realistic and feasible (p. 164-165).

Ways of using this sequence: At times you may simply keep the sequence in your mind, at others you may alert members to the steps and suggest it may be a useful structure to work through. It can make for variety to use sub-groups for some steps and pool the findings before going on to the next steps.

4. **Timing the discussion**

You need to consider how long people are likely to maintain their interest and concentration without a break. If people are tired, the quality of the discussion and decision-making will suffer.

You also need to check through your ideas in relation to the time they are likely to take and the time available. You may wish to jot the times down the margin of the agenda or your preparatory notes. Doing this will help you to see the relative importance of the various parts and possibly to amend the structure or methods. It can be helpful to have some idea of the alternatives which could be discussed if, in the eventuality, time unexpectedly runs short (p. 116).

5. **Notes and records**[25]

If notes are taken of the discussion, you have a choice between offering to make copies available to members or producing minutes or a record. The making of immediately available notes is described on page 103. Here, I distinguish between a record and minutes and outline the potential value of a record.

Minutes usually give brief details of the meeting and note decisions taken. A record is more than that: it is an orderly summarised account of the main points of the discussion; it traces the steps and stages; it gives the reasons and thinking underlying decisions; it may include a description of the interaction between members and a note of the processes and methods used.

Making this sort of record is demanding and time-consuming but has many advantages as a development tool:

- By objectifying and re-presenting what was said it enables members to do further work on the subject with less likelihood of repeating themselves or allowing the discussion to go round in circles.

- It helps members to realise that they and what they say, both as individuals and as a group, are being taken seriously. This promotes responsible participation and encourages people to use language accurately; it encourages a feeling of achievement and group solidarity.

- It provides useful research material: by structuring the records of a series of meetings an overall picture of the situation can be seen. This can lead to general insights and aid the planning process.

- It allows members to give themselves to the discussion without having to make notes, although some may wish to do so.

- It may clarify and sort out points of confusion or disagreement, and provide a basis for the team leader to suggest ways of moving on. This is particularly useful after an unsatisfactory meeting and gives members some hope of working through the chaos, conflict or impasse.

Skilled note-takers render an invaluable service to a group. Some people are able to take notes and join in the discussion but there is much to be gained from having an independent person who concentrates silently on getting down the main points. Note-takers need some basic skills in writing accurately and fast. Shorthand can be a disadvantage as it tempts the recorder to take down every word and needs translating before it can be used. The same difficulty attaches to the use of a tape recorder, although at times this may be useful.

The making of the record may be a task on which the note-taker and facilitator co-operate (p. 123).

IV. PREPARING THE PARTICIPANTS

1. **Orientation and prior thought**

A meeting can get off to a bad start when people arrive with expectations at variance with the objective. They may expect to be given answers or be told what to do, whereas you may want them to think and decide for themselves. Some may arrive at a meeting expecting it to be boring. Some may expect an argument ending with a win or lose vote, rather than a discussion in which people try to understand each other, make allowances and come to a consensus. Some may expect to sit back and be entertained or instructed, rather than contribute their own thoughts and feelings. Some may expect you to take their side in a dispute rather than explore the causes and work for an amicable solution. Something may prove difficult which people expected to be easy. The list of inappropriate expectations is endless. All this is a recipe for confusion, conflict, disappointment and frustration (p. 108).

Telling people beforehand what the meeting is about and, in general terms, how they will be expected to participate will help to minimise false expectations. This can be done verbally or in writing. The amount and kind of preparation you wish people to make depends among other things on the group, the subject matter, time available, your objective, and the type of meeting. At one end of the scale, participants may be asked to come with proposals, plans or information; to read something and reflect on it; to produce a paper; or to make notes beforehand; at the other, just to let certain ideas or questions 'go through their minds'. In either case it is important to stress the value of each individual's unique perspective and potential contribution.

When working with a group which does not know you it can be particularly valuable to make some contact beforehand. In correspondence, you could inform people about yourself, your attitudes to the task, and your way of working so that people arrive feeling positive towards you and the meeting. Or you may know one of their number who would give the group some verbal assurances on your behalf, either collectively or informally on the grapevine.

2. Convening a meeting

Arranging a mutually convenient date for a meeting can take a lot of time and effort but unless this is done some members may miss meeting after meeting because they are absent when the dates are fixed. A group with a large number of absentees not only loses their contributions but is likely to have an increasingly low morale because those present may feel the absences reflect the meeting's lack of worth or importance. This can often be avoided by fixing provisional dates and checking with absentees; by getting possible dates from absentees beforehand; by fixing several meetings well ahead; and by circulating the dates as soon as they are agreed.

When convening a meeting from scratch, by phone or letter, making a simple chart can expedite matters:

	Mon 4th	Wed 6th	Mon 11th	Tue 19th
JS	✓	✗	✓	✓
ER	✗	✓	✓	?
ON	✓	✓	✓	✗

CHECK LIST

Is there anything I can do or say beforehand which will help people to look forward to the meeting, to come ready and willing to participate and prepared to engage in the task? Do I need to introduce myself?

Can I do these things by post, by phone or face-to-face? through someone else, by a notice or by a paper or memorandum?

Do I need to say anything at this stage so participants are clear about their role and function in relation to the objective or task; for example, whether they are being consulted, are making decisions, etc. (p. 44)?

Do I need to make it clear that the various items of the agenda call for different approaches – some are for information, some for discussion, etc.?

What sort of preparation am I expecting of them? Is there anything I need to do or ask others to do in preparation for any specific items on the agenda? Any information we need to obtain? Any prior thinking and clarification? Is there anything I need to do or say to any particular individuals who have a special role to play?

Do I need to check up on attendance or send a reminder? What action do I need to take in relation to possible or known absentees? Would it help to get their views on any item?

Are there any dangers I need to guard against in talking to people outside the meeting? Asking yourself "Why do I want to talk to X?" can help you to identify your motives and clarify if a prior conversation with X is legitimate or not.

V. PREPARING THE VENUE, RESOURCES, AND PRACTICALITIES

Preparation of the venue may be a simple matter if you are on home ground but it can be problematic if you are using other people's premises. In either case a caretaker, should there be one, can be a key person in generating a welcoming or hostile atmosphere. You would be well advised to try and visit unknown premises beforehand, both to make contact with whoever is responsible and negotiate what you need, so that the practical arrangements go smoothly.

In preparing a room for a meeting it can be helpful to consider the following factors:

- The atmosphere and decor of a room: most people will be affected by it even though they may not realise it. Floral or other symbolic décor may seem a minor point but it can be helpful to have something on which people can feast their eyes if they become bored or tired.

- People usually prefer the sort of seating arrangement they are used to and so it can be helpful to explain the reason behind any change (p. 155).

- The use of a table or tables: when people have lots of papers to refer to, it can help to sit round a table or have low tables nearby to rest papers on. Sitting in a large circle can be intimidating: putting a few low coffee tables around can break up the space.

- Arrangement of chairs: everyone needs to see, hear and participate as appropriate. Do people need to be able to see each other or the board or visual aids? Seating in large groups is discussed on page 155; what about heating, lighting and ventilation: ignoring these factors can be disastrous.

- The direction in which the majority of people will face: minimise distractions such as windows, bookshelves, pictures, mirrors and people arriving late.

- The type of chairs to be used in relation to the function people will be engaged in: low and comfy chairs help people to relax but may be too relaxing; hard upright chairs may be distractingly uncomfortable. Have sufficient similarity or dissimilarity to prevent anyone appearing singular because they are in the best seat or the only one of its kind or colour.

- Availability of everything likely to be needed: notes, papers, handouts, books, overhead projector, screen, felt pens, board or flip chart, chalk and duster, Blu-Tack, etc.; and information about members, the length of the meeting, any breaks, and so on. It is worth making one's own check list.

These all carry non-verbal signals (p. 110). Setting the scene in these ways is a prelude to encouraging and supporting members in verbal and non-verbal ways on arrival and throughout the meeting.

CHECK LIST

Do I need to take any action in relation to:

- the venue: address, telephone number, directions for finding it . . . ?

- parking, entering the building, cloakrooms, security, stairs/lift facilities, other groups using the building or sharing facilities, clearing away . . . ?

- preparation of the room, refreshments . . . ?

- caretaker or those responsible for the premises?

- availability of tables, appropriate chairs, overhead projector, electric points . . . ?

1. T.R. Batten, *op.cit.*, Note 1, p. 22.
2. This section is based on the work of T.R. Batten and George Lovell.
3. See 'Indispensable Self-Esteem' by James I. Gill in *Human Development*, Vol. One, No. Three, Fall 1980.
4. Ira Progoff, after studying with Jung, developed journalling as 'a tool for life'. See *At a Journal Workshop* and *Process Meditation* (Dialogue House Library NY). Information about Progoff Intensive Journal Workshops can be obtained from William Hewett SJ, Campion Hall, Brewer Street, Oxford OX1 1QS, tel. 01865 286 100, fax 01865 286 148.
5. Tony Buzan, *Use Your Head* (BBC 1982), p. 103.
6. Gabriele Lurser Rico, *Writing the Natural Way* (J.P. Tarcher Inc. Los Angeles, Houghton Miffin Co., Boston 1983), p. 28.
7. George Lovell has written a handout which includes these points.
8. I am indebted to George Lovell for this distinction.
9. Rudyard Kipling, *The Complete Verse* (Kyle Cathie Ltd 1990).
10. E. Mayo 'Hawthorn and the Western Electric Company' in *The Social Problems of an Industrial Society* (Routledge and Kegan Paul 1949).
11. Bernard Kilroy outlines this method in *Collaboration in Ministry* an unpublished thesis for the Avec Diploma in Church and Community Development 1991.
12. Two fascinating books relating to developing our creativity are *Drawing on the Right Side of the Brain* by Betty Edwards (Fontana/Collins 1979) and *Writing Naturally* by Gabriele Lurser Rico, *op.cit.*; Walter Wink has applied the insights of this research to bible study in *Transforming Bible Study* (SCM Press 1980).
13. George Lovell, *Diagrammatic Modelling: An Aid to Theological Reflection in Church and Community Development Work* (William Temple Foundation Occasional Paper No. 4, 1980 reprinted as an Avec Publication in 1991), p. 16. Lovell draws on the work of Ian T. Ramsey *Models and Theology*, The Whidden Lectures for 1963 (Oxford University Press 1984).
14. I am indebted to George Lovell for this and the next two illustrations.
15. For an example see *Churches and Communities: An Approach to Development in the Local Church* by George Lovell and Catherine Widdicombe (The Search Press 1978), p. 140.
16. George Lovell, *Analysis and Design: A Handbook for Practitioners and Consultants in Church and Community Work*, (Burns & Oates 1994) pp. 179-184.
17. For an example see Lovell and Widdicombe, *op.cit.*, p. 142.
18. See a useful chapter on 'Role-Play' in *New Ways to Better Meetings* by F. Strauss and B. Strauss (The Viking Press 1957), p. 91.
19. See T.R. Batten 1967 *op. cit.* p. 100 for a useful section on the value and use of role play.
20. A method of de-briefing: a) ask each person to make a final statement as the characer they have taken on; b) invite them to become themselves by moving physically to another place; c) ask them to say their own name, followed by something they are looking forward to.
21. Anthony de Mello, *Sadhana, A Way to God* (Image Books, Doubleday NY 1985), p. 73. See also Walter Wink *op.cit.*, Note 12.
22. This draws heavily on the work of T.R. Batten 1967 *op.cit.*, and George Lovell's further elaboration 'Notes on Exploring Causes and Sources in Problem Solving' (An Avec handout) based on the work of L. Amadeo and J.S. Gill, 'Managing Anger and Hostility', *Human Development*, Vol. 1 No. 3 Fall 1980, and P. Walzlawick, J. Weakland and R. Fisch, *Problem Formation and Problem Resolution* (W.W. Naughton 1974).
23. Erich Fromm, *To Have or To Be* (Jonathan Cape 1978), p. 21.
24. Edward de Bono, *The Five Day Course in Thinking* (Penguin 1967).
25. Much of this section is based on the work of George Lovell and his late colleague, Dorothy Houshold.

PART THREE

Conducting a meeting

This section falls into three parts:
the opening of a meeting,
conducting discussion during it,
and bringing the meeting to a conclusion.

I. OPENING A MEETING

What happens during the first few minutes of a meeting is crucial: it can relax and reassure both you and the group or do the exact opposite. Among the group members there will be feelings and attitudes to which you are not privy and which will encourage or inhibit the quality of their participation. One or more people may be shy and insecure and afraid of saying the wrong thing; others may be bored, defensive or preoccupied. You need to do what you can to mobilise positive feelings and counteract any negative ones. Noticing your own reactions at the start of meetings you attend will sensitise you and inform your introduction. There are several factors to be taken into account. They are not in any particular order.

1. **Your manner**

Whatever your feelings, whether they range from extreme nervousness to over-confidence, or from boredom to enthusiasm, they are likely to colour the way you hold yourself and speak. In order to prevent them having an adverse effect on the group you could try the suggestions below.

If you are nervous or bored:
- relax your body, smile, look as though you are pleased to be there; pause and take a deep breath; try not to talk too fast;
- concentrate on helping members of the group to get over any nervousness or negativity *they* may be experiencing;
- level with the group: for example, admit you are nervous or find the task somewhat daunting. This could be unwise if members are likely to lose confidence in you or take advantage of you, but generally speaking it encourages members who may themselves be nervous.

If you tend to be over-confident or over-enthusiastic:
- avoid a boisterous or hearty delivery;
- be tentative in your approach;
- avoid too many jokes;
- try to suit the way you speak to the mood of the group.

In deciding what would be helpful, you need to take into account what would be appropriate to a particular group. A more formal group might expect you to stand or sit upright, or even lean slightly forward to indicate your acceptance of their formal standards.

2. **Your opening gambit**

Ideally, the introductory remarks will not only put members at their ease but quicken their interest and stimulate them to participate. Some people find it useful to draft their opening remarks and to check them out with a colleague or by mentally standing in the shoes of those who will hear them (p. 74).

3. **Forming a working relationship**

Whether or not people know you, it is important to form the sort of relationship which will be effective in relation to the task ahead. People may see you as a personal friend, in a management or subordinate position, as an ally or in opposition. They may not know you at all or know you well, you may feel only too well! All this will affect their motivation. Below I list some key things I have found useful. Forming a relationship in more difficult situations with groups which are reluctant and hostile is discussed in Part Five (pp. 140 and 141).

- Explain your way of working, what you are trying to do at this particular meeting and what is expected of the members. With groups that do not know me I like to explain that "I see this as a collaborative exercise in which we are each responsible for our own thinking and learning but in which we also try to help each other to think, and in which we build on each other's ideas and explore them rather than argue against them, so we grapple with the task together." You may suggest some basic 'ground rules' for discussion and agreement; for instance, based on those on pages 37 and 38.

- If people know you have strong views about a topic, they may need to be told that you want all views considered and you do not intend to 'sell' your own.

- If people know each other well, suggest they listen to each other "as though you have not met before". This can help you and the rest of the group to see and appreciate people in a new light.

- Make your position clear: for example, you have no intention of putting undue pressure on people but intend to use the time in a way which will be productive and enjoyable for everyone. If you have been asked in by a person in authority rather than the group itself, let them know by implication that you are not there to get them to do something on someone else's behalf. You have your own independence and integrity (p. 175).

4. Introducing yourself and other people

If you are working with a group to whom you are a stranger (p. 175) it is helpful to establish some common bond or link as soon as possible, for example, by referring to some place or person they also know, or to an event or experience which they know about or have participated in. Introducing people who do not know each other is considered in Part One (p. 27) as is welcoming a new member (p. 30).

5. Time

Meetings which start late can give the impression that the subject of the meeting is unimportant, but to start on the dot if several people have not arrived can make for bad feeling and it can be difficult to help them catch up. It may be useful to discuss the predicament with the group or negotiate a few minutes' grace.

Again, people will be encouraged to enter into discussion if they know such important details as when the meeting will end, when there will be a break, what arrangements, if any, have been made for refreshments and whether or not notes or a record of the meeting will be made available (p. 123). It can be helpful if your co-worker or a group member acts as time keeper and agrees to alert the group ten minutes before the end. All this can reassure people, help them to concentrate on the task and galvanise them into getting it completed.

6. Setting the scene

In introducing the topic or subject of the meeting it is useful to situate it within the context of the on-going life of the team or group and show how and why it has arisen. This background enables members to look more carefully and critically at the stated objective of the meeting (p. 46). For example, working with a voluntary group it could be useful to outline its history in diagrammatic form, when and why it started, key events or activities, its links with other similar organisations or its headquarters, the context in which it is working; and then state where it is now, what questions, tasks or decisions it is facing (p. 68). Clearly, this all needs to be checked out as people may well perceive things differently. Doing this helps to base the discussion on a common understanding of what has brought people together at this point in time.

7. Agreeing on the topic and aim of the meeting

Members of a group or team are more likely to work effectively if they see the relevance or value of the topic or task and agree to devote time to it. This you need to ascertain at the start. As has been discussed on page 55, your introduction needs to be clear and reasonably succinct: if you are obscure or wordy you may well induce boredom, but if you say too little, people may not have time to grasp what the meeting will be about. Should there be some reluctance, this needs to be explored (p. 139). Likewise, if an alternative subject is suggested, and the group is free to do so, you need to decide together whether or not to change direction and if and when to deal with the original task. If the decision is to change you will need to work out how best to tackle the new subject.

Just as establishing objectives is an essential part of your own preparation for a meeting, so checking out the group's objectives and either changing, amending or agreeing to them is necessary at the start of a meeting (p. 46). In meetings which are particularly significant, it is helpful to write up the objective, explain it and ask people to discuss it with their neighbours. Is it clear and comprehensive? Are they willing to work to it? In less formal or important meetings a verbal agreement may be sufficient. Formulating and checking an agenda for more formal groups and committees is considered in Part Six (p. 151).

8. Clarifying the role and function of participants

It is important to clarify the role and function of the members so they can participate effectively. This is considered on page 44.

9. Confidentiality

If the subject matter of a meeting is likely for any reason to be confidential, it is important to say a word about confidentiality and ascertain with the members at the start how they wish to handle the confidentiality of the discussion. Confidentiality is considered on page 45.

You may, as facilitator, have confidential information not available to the group: for instance, if a member has confided in you. Should you be operating under a constraint of this kind, you may be able to let the group know without breaking confidence by simply saying something like "I have some information which I am not free to divulge." Clearly, you would only need to do this if the information you have affects your contribution. It should not be experienced by the group as manipulation or a way of exerting power.

10. **Latecomers and absentees**

When you have to start without people, or if some are absent, it can be useful to mention them by name and possibly ask different members of the group to be responsible for reporting on the meeting or talking it through with them later (p. 125). If late comers arrive when the discussion is in full flow, a word or gesture will help them to feel welcome. It may be appropriate to suggest they get their breath back and say you will help them catch up in a few minutes (p. 27). In which case, it is important to remember to do so!

After your introduction, people should:

- be clear about and agree the objective of the meeting;
- know what sort of participation is expected of them;
- feel they know something about other members;
- be motivated to participate;
- know when the meeting will end;
- be agreed, should this be necessary, about the confidential nature of the discussion;
- know whether or not a record or notes will subsequently be made available.

II. **DURING A MEETING**

The key functions of a facilitator aiming to promote a thoughtful and creative exchange of views were described on pages 37 and 38. They were about creating the right atmosphere, getting agreement and clarity on the subject matter, structuring the discussion, considering all ideas objectively, openly and critically and providing periodic summaries and information as appropriate. Below, more specific aspects are discussed.

1. **Using, not misusing your preparatory work**

Your preparatory thinking should help you to introduce and structure the discussion (p. 49) and contribute your own ideas as appropriate (p. 91). This section suggests ways of making the most of your preparation and some pitfalls to be avoided.

Testing your structure. It is wise to consider how casually or how stringently you will test the structure with the group. Some people would find too clear or complex a structure intimidating, others stimulating. For example, with an unsophisticated group, too thorough a testing at the start could prove daunting. All that may be required is a clear statement of the question or area you suggest focusing on at this stage of the discussion. However, with issues of crucial importance, thoroughly checking out with members that the particular questions or tasks are acceptable and likely to be productive may well prevent wasted time and effort and consequent frustration.

In testing out your proposed structure, be tentative, ensure that it makes sense to people and is likely to provide a useful framework for exploring the issue. "I've been thinking about how we can best get into this subject. Can I suggest a structure which I think could help us? Please think about it critically." In doing this it is important to 'work to the group' by listening, responding, and exploring their comments. You need to listen, in particular, for the question or comment which seems off the point or which does not fit into your suggested structure. Such contributions, taken seriously, often reveal a new dimension to the subject or a more effective way of approaching it. However, this does not necessarily mean jettisoning your preparation: check whether there is any link between the two. You can do this as you listen or you may raise it: "I had thought we would need to think about these questions . . . but we've come up with others. What would be of most use?"

Remaining flexible. The structure has to fit the group. Too rigid a structure can prevent people from contributing because what they have to say does not appear to them to 'fit in' anywhere; too loose a structure and the discussion becomes discursive and unsatisfying and encourages tangential ideas. Some people just may not find it helpful and come up with another suggestion halfway through the discussion. The danger is that, having invested a lot of time and energy in thinking up a structure, you keep too rigidly to it and try to fit what is being said on to predetermined 'hooks' in your own mind and so manipulate or direct the discussion. Try to remain flexible and sensitive to the needs of the group, prepared at any stage to adjust the structure, add to it or even scrap it altogether if it is proving unhelpful.

You may become aware at a later stage that the discussion has gone along different lines from those envisaged. If you want to do a quick check of your notes, you could say, "I've become completely absorbed in what we've all been talking about. Can I just have a couple of minutes to look back over my notes to see if there are any questions we should have covered . . . ?" At the same time you could suggest they ask themselves if anything has been forgotten.

As my confidence has grown, I find that I am able increasingly to work to the group as the discussion unfolds and so my preparatory thinking is called upon as appropriate and does not obtrude.

Sharing your ideas: Some facilitators, if they are outsiders to the group and therefore unaffected by decisions made, seek to be neutral in relation to the content of the discussion and contribute nothing themselves. However, as facilitator you are a resource in the group with your ideas and insights to share. How far and when to do this depends on the situation and the topic. To share too much, too early, can preempt discussion; too little, and people may legitimately suspect you of holding back and possibly 'knowing the answers'; too late, and your ideas may appear to cap theirs. At times, I find that withholding too much of my preparatory thinking can give me a feeling of pretence when I am aiming for co-operative exploration of ideas between myself and members.

CHECK LIST ON STRUCTURES AND
CONTRIBUTING IDEAS

Will it be most helpful to set out a suggested structure and check it all out at the start or check it out bit by bit as we come to it?

How can I best use my own preparatory thinking?

How much of it should I share at the start? How are people likely to react to me setting out a structure for the meeting?

When should I contribute my ideas? How can I get people to consider my ideas critically?

---

2. **Helping people to think** (p. 190)

Just as we cannot do people's thinking for them, neither can we make them think. What we can do is to motivate and encourage, provide opportunities, skills and techniques. After Gillian Stamp had been working with a group of Aborigines for a period, one gave her the answer to the question he had earlier asked her, "I can tell you what you have brought. You have brought me tools for my head."

Most people make use of efficient tools if they are to hand and they want to do a particular job. If a group wants to think through something, the job of the facilitator is comparatively easy. It is harder and may be extremely difficult to get people to think about things which they do not want to think about, things which we believe they need to think about for their own good. Given that we cannot force them to do so, even if we wanted to, what can be done to help, encourage and motivate people in this situation?

To begin with, it is necessary to realise that people think very differently from each other. Ideally, a meeting should contain opportunities for people to think in a variety of ways so that the thinking resources of the whole group are all brought into play. As well as quick thinkers and slow thinkers, there are those who think more abstractly and theoretically, others who are more practical and down to earth; some people are logical and systematic, others think laterally, pragmatically, or intuitively. Few of us make full use of our innate thinking abilities: our education is likely to have developed that side of our brain which is logical and rational rather than the more creative and intuitive (p. 67).

Among the things which are likely to help motivate any group to think when it is hard work to do so, are the following:

- Admit that thinking can be demanding and hard work as well as rewarding. Gently challenge people to commit themselves to it for the next hour or however long the meeting will take.

- Acknowledge that you have at times to struggle and discipline yourself to think.

- Be positive and hopeful about the outcome. A man, asked to list things which he knew he should think about, said afterwards, "I made a list of things I half think about and when I got to No. 6 I put down something I'd not previously been conscious of."

- Find an introduction which is immediately clear and compelling (p. 55).

- Ask them why they do not want to think about a certain thing? Explore with them any potential benefits for doing so and any pitfalls to be avoided.

- Share your concerns about their need to think about a particular issue. Avoid sounding judgmental or superior.

3. **Questions and questioning**

Asking questions is an art and it is central to promoting thought and discussion. On page 55 six areas of questioning were described: searching, formulating, timing, testing, asking and reassuring. The first four, which particularly need to be thought about when preparing for a meeting, were discussed in detail (pp. 56-58). Other aspects to take into account during a meeting are outlined below.

- *Timing your questions*: Some questions may be more difficult to ask or respond to than others. It is useful to ask oneself, "When is the best moment to ask this question? When is the person or group most likely to be open to consider it?"

  Sometimes you may want to encourage the slow pondering of a question as people grapple with it. It can help to give people time to think before replying by suggesting, "Can we pause for a minute to think about this?" You need to follow your own suggestion: too often I have seen facilitators looking vacant while others do the thinking! At other times, a quicker tempo as people brainstorm, may be more appropriate and encourage creativity (p. 98). Varying the pace can be useful.

  Some issues are likely to be so crucial to the members that they need to be warned in advance and given a few days or longer to mull them over or discuss them informally amongst themselves.

  If I know that a member is reticent and afraid to speak, possibly overawed by the others, my first question to him will come later in the meeting and be worded in a non-threatening way: "Is there anything you want to add, John, at this stage?" or "Does anyone who has not spoken, want to add anything?"

- *Asking questions*: However stimulating and well formulated the question, the way in which it is asked is crucial and will be affected by what is going on in me as a person and what is going on in the group.

  My manner will be influenced by what I myself feel about the task or topic and this will be coloured, among other things, by my past experience. Not only have I to show I am genuinely interested in the question and pre-pared to work at it myself, but I also have to believe that the group is likely to be interested, and is capable of working on it. By the way I ask the question, I can build people's confidence and motivate them to grapple with it.

  I also need to be aware, as far as possible, of people's preoccupations, attitudes, and feelings, particularly any which may relate to the subject or any likely to take the discussion off course, or cause difficulties. One or more people may be afraid to speak out, be present under duress, consider the topic irrelevant, want to score points, or demonstrate their expertise, be coping with emotional stress, be exhausted, or habitually play a certain role in the group. Clearly, however sensitive one is, it is not possible to make a totally accurate assessment of all this, but picking up any clues as to their feelings and attitudes will help you to take them into account and put your questions in a way people are most likely to find sympathetic. For instance, it could be that members of a work team hoping to discuss a particular topic are asked by the management to give their views as part of a consultative process. They may resent this 'take over' of their discussion. You might acknowledge the situation openly. "We had planned to talk about x and now we've been asked to give our ideas on y. I imagine some of us are not all that keen on the switch but without being un-co-operative we can't ignore this request and it is something which should ultimately be of benefit to all of us in the firm. Can we make the best of it? If we put our minds to it, we'll probably finish and then be able to get back to our own programme next time." In this way the facilitator aims to make an informal contract to work on it, despite any disappointment or negative feelings (p. 163).

- *Re-assuring as you question*: In the classroom situation you have probably experienced, when replying to a question, that your questioner was seeking a particular answer or is not really listening to anything else you say. All the more necessary, therefore, when asking a question to reassure people that their contribution really is wanted and that what they say will be considered. They are more likely to think hard about the question if you are seen to be taking them and their contribution seriously. This is easier said than done particularly if the ideas and answers are not in accord with your own thinking and experience (p. 43). But if you accept some point and ignore others, people will quickly lose heart.

It is not enough for you to listen and respond to what is being said; others need to listen and respond as well. I try to create this atmosphere by showing that I, at least, am listening to every word, both by my non-verbal signals such as keeping my eyes on the speaker, leaning forward, giving a nod or smile (p. 110), and also by my verbal response, which may be to clarify the last contribution of one or more speakers or summarise periodically.

4. **Working with a colleague**

The tasks of a co-worker in relation to a meeting were briefly outlined on page 61 with a view to helping you decide whether or not to ask a colleague to work with you in a particular meeting. These tasks are amplified below. Evaluating a meeting with a co-worker is discussed on page 131.

- *Supporting and backing up the facilitator.* This may well entail such things as asking questions which lead the facilitator to clarify or add to what has been said or to check out a decision, making suggestions, assessing whether the facilitator is picking up what is being said, etc. The co-worker needs to be tentative in making interventions: "I'm not sure how people feel about this. I'm a bit perplexed about that. This is going to entail quite a bit of work, is this all right? Do you need more time to consider that? I'm not clear what is being said about. . . ."

  Co-workers need to keep an eye on the pace. When they think the discussion is going too fast, or too slowly, it can be helpful to say "I'm finding the pace a bit fast" or "Are we ready to go on to another point?" In fact, being prepared, as necessary, to perform any of the facilitator's functions summarised on pages 37 and 38.

  A colleague can make a highly significant contribution if and when the facilitator gets into an argument or is put under pressure, or appears to be taking sides. The co-worker can then become the 'facilitator' and try to get the issues discussed objectively by helping all concerned to explore the ideas being put forward.

- *Supporting and encouraging group members*: The co-worker observes what is happening, whether or not members are interested, if someone is trying to speak, or if anyone is upset in any way. The very way in which the co-worker listens to what is being said encourages a listening attitude in others.

- *The content*: The co-worker can have a check list to refer to during the discussion or before the end so that any necessary points or questions are raised (p. 55). Co-workers may also contribute to the discussion, keeping in mind the points raised on page 91 'Sharing your ideas'.

- *Timing*: It may be the co-worker's task to be time-keeper and remind the facilitator and members of the group how the time is going (p. 77).

As the meeting proceeds, the co-worker may find it useful to jot down any points to be discussed with the facilitator afterwards (p. 131).

From all this it might be thought that co-workers have a very active role and certainly they need to be alert and actively engaged in listening and thinking, but they may intervene very little. Any intervention is made as expeditiously as possible with an eye to encouraging and facilitating the discussion. The role therefore calls for sensitivity and tact. A relationship of trust between facilitator and co-worker is crucial. In case difficulties arise between you, it is important to come to an understanding beforehand that you will work through any such problems outside the meeting. While in the meeting, the members and the discussion come first.

QUESTIONS FOR THE CO-WORKER

Before a meeting:

Am I clear what is expected of me in relation to the facilitator? group members? the material? time-keeping?

During the meeting:

Is the facilitator getting hold of significant points?

Are his summaries clear and comprehensive and balanced?

Is he overlooking something?

Is someone 'trying to get in'? confused?

Is interest waning? Is anyone looking bored or negative in any way?

---

5. Engendering objectivity

Increasing the objectivity with which ideas and opinions are expressed and considered is a key function of the facilitator. No one can ever achieve complete objectivity: we receive, understand and assess information which comes to us from the outside world through the medium of our person, and we have become who we are through what we have made of our previous experience. We are each unique and see things in a unique way. Inevitably, therefore, to a greater or lesser extent, consciously or unconsciously, we react emotionally to what we hear and see. Hence the richness of human intercourse and its potential dangers and the need, when facilitating a meeting, to endeavour to increase your objectivity and that of group members. In this way, you promote the exploration of ideas rather than arguing over them.

In order to increase objectivity, all contributions need to be given a fair hearing, treated seriously and taken into account. People are more likely to feel confident to express themselves in the knowledge that they will be supported and not made to feel small. In this, your intention is of utmost importance: without a sincere intention to get all ideas considered openly and critically the suggestions below become mere gimmicks; with it, the occasional failure is more likely to be forgiven.

Help people to take account of their feelings and attitudes

Try to be aware of what is happening within yourself (p. 40), within the individuals and between them as the discussion proceeds. By being alert to non-verbal signals you may pick up what is being felt or thought but not expressed (p. 110). By tentatively asking questions about what you think you are discerning, you may help people to be in touch with their feelings and take them into account.

Control your emotional involvement (p. 43)

When, as facilitator, you have strong feelings and views about the matter under discussion there is a danger of persuading or manipulating people into accepting your ideas without critically examining them. To avoid, this you might, at the start of the meeting:

- encourage people to raise questions or disagree by talking overtly to the group about the potential dangers e.g., "I'm finding it very difficult to see this objectively", "Please listen critically to what I am saying, I may not be summarising the situation accurately. . . ."

- help everyone to objectify the issues: "Can we all try to stand back from this now and see it from a distance. . . ."
- time your contribution and express yourself tentatively so that your ideas are submitted to the same objective and critical scrutiny as those of other people (p. 91). Try to make it easy for people to raise questions or disagree.

Being open about your emotional involvement in the issue can increase empathy and understanding between you and the group and help to build up a relationship of trust.

Present ideas visually

This can apply both to the facilitator and group. Writing up ideas so all can see them helps to ensure that points are not lost or repeated, and can be seen in relation to others being made. The very fact that an idea is put 'out there' helps to increase objectivity. A black or white board, flip chart, overhead projector, or sheet of paper round which everyone sits, may be used. Although most people find diagrams useful, it is worth remembering that they do not appeal to everyone, in fact, some people can react negatively. With this in mind their use can be introduced by saying, "Do you mind if I put up this diagram as it helps me to think?" "This may help some people. Can I try?" This is particularly important where the use of diagrams is not customary.

In using a board or flip chart, avoid standing in a dominating position or becoming more interested in the board than the group. (Reviewing your use of the board afterwards, alone or with others, can increase your proficiency.) If you have no board or decide not to use one, it is possible to use your hands to point out separate ideas, 'writing in the air' as it were. Participants may need encouragement to use chalk or pens themselves and these should be within reach of everyone.

The value and use of diagrams is considered on page 66.

Brainstorming

The rules I have found most useful for brainstorming are:

(a) Allow people a minute or two to think.

(b) List all points on a board or flip chart. This is done as quickly as possible without any discussion except to clarify a point. Above all there must be no criticism or denigration of any point at this stage.

(c) When ideas run dry, have a further pause while people reflect on the total list.

(d) After this any of the following may be appropriate:
- start at the top and discuss each point;
- get agreement on the 'two' or 'five' most important points and discuss those;
- cross out points which are clearly not feasible in the situation;
- divide into sub-groups and get each to discuss, assess or list pros and cons of one or more points. Listen to each report and discuss in plenary.

Note and assess all contributions on their merits

An idea is not more or less good according to who contributed it or the number of people who hold it. It needs to be explored objectively. If a course of action needs to be decided upon, try listing the pros and cons and the likely positive and negative effects of every alternative. If an idea put forward would clearly be more appropriately dealt with at a later stage, note it by 'putting it on a hook', but remember to return to it when the time comes or people will suspect you of avoiding the question or issue.

Depersonalise ideas

Refer to ideas in a way which does not link them with their contributors. It is easier to be objective about 'Idea 1' and 'Idea 2' than about John's idea and Joan's idea. It also increases objectivity if, when sub-groups report their findings on large sheets of paper, each is labelled A, B, C, etc. Encourage people to refer to them as 'Paper A' rather than say "Our group said". Ideally, ideas once contributed belong to the whole group and are there to be explored and examined, not attacked or defended.

Ensure understanding before critical assessment

Ensure that a contribution is clearly understood before it is critically considered. This is especially important when emotive issues are discussed.

Re-word contributions

When jargon or emotive language is used you may need to repeat what has been said in other terms to increase objectivity. It is also useful to do so when contributions are made forcibly, timidly, or when the person concerned is someone whom others habitually disregard. It is important to check by word or glance with the person concerned that you are expressing their point accurately.

6. Keeping to the point

Discussion can wander from the point for many reasons and, at times, it can be appropriate to allow it to do so. For instance, some people may need to express their feelings or share information about something before they can concentrate on the matter in hand. It can be difficult, when following a conversation, to know whether or not it is on the issue: I often find that the contributors see a connection which I have missed. Judging whether or not to intervene and how best to do so, is a question I constantly struggle with and which I do not always get right (p. 113). There is no infallible guide but I have found the following have, on various occasions, helped me to minimise 'red herrings':

- Ensure that people are agreed about what is to be discussed and why: people are unlikely to keep to the point if they do not know what it is or do not want to discuss it (p. 88).

- Have a clear structure, so people can see where the discussion is going. At times as people talk, a way of re-structuring it will occur to the facilitator and can be tentatively introduced "to help us move forward on this" (p. 90).

- Keep in mind both the objective of the discussion (p. 46) and the overall structure so you can keep the discussion moving: when a point has been exhausted or dealt with sufficiently, summarise, check for agreement and move to the next point (p. 111).

- Be alert to diversions and the introduction of lengthy anecdotes: "I remember when . . . " which can quickly take the discussion into other realms.

When the discussion has become discursive and you want to do something about it, rather than brusquely calling people to order, it can be helpful to point out that "we seem to have wandered on to another topic". This may be enough to bring the discussion back to the point or it may be useful to ask, "What do you think, should we continue on this or go back to the subject we were originally talking about?" Or you could say, "I am not sure how what we are talking about relates to the issue we met to work at. Where are we?" Thus you make the group responsible for its agenda rather than assuming responsibility yourself.

7. **Sub-groups**

The potential value of sub-groups, the various methods of forming them, and ways in which they could report back, have already been discussed in the section on preparing for a meeting (p. 61). Here we consider introducing sub-groups, briefing and supporting them, and receiving their reports.

Introducing sub-groups

At its most informal it can be useful to suggest people have a word with their neighbours. At the other end of the scale, you may want to explain why you are suggesting the use of sub-groups and check out that people are willing to work in them. If you have decided who will belong to each sub-group, it is helpful to explain why you have done so and the criteria you have used. e.g., "so that everyone is with people from the same area" or "so each group has people from every department", or "there is a good cross section of age, sex, denominations, experience, etc." Occasionally people will resist working in sub-groups: they may have had a bad experience in the past or not want to get down to work. Suggesting people "talk to their neighbours" or go into groups "just for ten minutes" can help to dispel resistance. However, it can be dysfunctional to make people go into groups if they are set against it. At times I have found it useful to explore why people dislike sub-groups and this has helped us together to find a way round the difficulty.

Briefing sub-groups

This is of cardinal importance and makes for success or failure. Below are some suggestions:

- Ensure that the task is acceptable and one which people feel able to tackle: check it out thoroughly and be prepared to amend it or reword it.

- Ensure the task or question is utterly clear by writing it up or putting it on a slip of paper for each person or group.

- Check people understand the task and that all is well by going round the groups after a few minutes.

- As appropriate suggest how members might work together so that all are able to participate. You could variously suggest that:

  - people pause for personal reflection for 2-5 minutes before they start work;

- all ideas are pooled and listed before any are discussed and critically assessed or amended and amalgamated; or members simply listen to each other without comment or discussion and only questions for clarification are asked. This is especially useful for people who are not used to group discussion: to be listened to attentively can build up self-confidence (p. 137);

- people focus on identifying a few key points rather than compiling a long list;

- one member helps the group to work through the task and keep to the point and to time.

- Suggest how long people are likely to need and negotiate longer or shorter as necessary once the groups are under way.

- Ask each group to appoint someone to report back and give some guidance on the sort of feedback you want, e.g., verbal, written on a large or small sheet, diagrammatic, using a particular structure, giving only a few key points, etc. (p. 64).

- If there are absent members, sub-groups may be asked to put themselves in their shoes and contribute any thoughts or feelings they think the absentees might have.

Supporting sub-groups

You may leave the groups to work on their own or it may be useful after some time to see how they are getting on and whether they need help.

When groups have a difficult task and a good length of time to work at it, it can be helpful to negotiate a roving consultancy role: "If you want my help, I am available. I will come round periodically and sit in on your discussion. In this case if you want my help ask for it; if you want me to leave, just say you are getting on all right and do not need me. If I remain I may keep silent or I may make a comment or raise a question. Is this all right?"

It is also useful to go round a few minutes before time is up to warn people and if necessary extend the time at this stage. This is usually more acceptable to people than 'issuing orders' to all groups from the centre of the room. It may be necessary to negotiate more time or, if some or all have not finished the task, to suggest people bring what ideas they have "so we can see where we've got to".

Reporting back

Methods of reporting back are described on page 64. Whatever method is chosen it can be useful as appropriate to:

- check with the other members of the sub-group that they are satisfied with their report; they may want to add or amend something. A more thorough checking needs to be done if a collation has been made of the work of all the groups;

- ensure that a report is understood before it is discussed: begin by asking for 'questions of clarification'. Possibly hear all the reports in this way before discussing them separately or together;

- pause between the presentation of each report and suggest people jot down any comments, feelings, questions or simply "what strikes you";

- suggest people listen to each report and try to make a comprehensive summary as they do so. Most people find this sort of collating difficult: it is an important function of a facilitator and a skill worth acquiring;

- ask for one point at a time from each group in turn, asking other groups to contribute anything similar to what is being offered: thus points are collated by the worker in turn and it can be useful to put these on a board or flip chart. This avoids the situation in which the last group to report has nothing new to say;

- discuss each point critically as it is contributed or get out all the points and put them in priority order before considering each one;

- display the findings of each group and allow time for people to study them and possibly make their own summary or jot down general comments or comments in relation to a particular question, e.g., "as you look at the various ideas, ask yourself how you would respond if you were a person who likes the *status quo.*"

It is vital that people are clear as to what is expected of them when the reporting back process begins.

8. Note-taking and making records[1]

The value of a written record and discussion of the sort of notes required has been outlined on page 77. This section gives some basic instructions for note-takers and discusses the importance of introducing note-takers to the group. The writing up of a structured record is described on page 123.

Note-takers will need plenty of paper on a clipboard and something to write with: it can be useful to have a coloured biro or two. They need to sit un-obtrusively and be able to see the flip chart or board and all members of the group. Notes usually include:

- a list of members and facilitators present;

- a note about the topic and why it is being discussed;

- diagrams with explanatory notes; it is wise to write in full any abbrev-iations used on a diagram;

- a note of all the points made but not every word or sentence. Amusing or significant phrases may be taken verbatim. Except in notes which will be made immediately available, note down the initials of speakers although in any final record these may be omitted (p. 124);

- a mention of the kind of discussion, e.g. discursive, lively, etc.;

- any decisions made and a note about who will take what action and when;

- questions or outstanding points for further consideration.

The more one can put the notes into some kind of shape or pattern as the discussion flows, the better: it makes it easier to pick out key points and build on the discussion next time.

Immediately available notes

This requires a legible hand and quick mind in order to capture the main points and make a succinct summary as the discussion progresses. If notes like this can be made efficiently, particularly of shorter meetings, a lot of time is saved, but generally speaking they are not so useful for on-going discussion in a group. In addition to the briefing noted above, the recorder may find it is helpful to:

- use a black pen and A4 paper so the notes can be photocopied after the meeting;

- write so there is enough room to add in later points. It can be helpful to: leave a wide margin on the left
    for headings
    for annotating
    for questions or notes which occur later.

- underline in different ways: ————   – – – – – –   ════

- put HEADINGS in caps or lower case in text or in margin;
- have some clear numbering system. For example, I, II, III, . . . 1, 2, 3, . . . A, B, C, . . . (a) (b), . . . (i), (ii), . . . (iii), Keep the sequence and use constant;
- number each page at the bottom and date the work;
- use blobs to mark new points or make a list with dashes before each point;
- use question marks to indicate questions being asked;
- use an arrow to show related points or to indicate all that went before which led to this conclusion/or question/or summary;
- provide a key for any abbreviations used in the notes;
- put an asterisk in the margin for points which need to be picked up later;
- write ACTION in the margin for tasks to be done.

Introducing the note-taker

It is important for the group to understand why notes are being taken and what is going to happen to them afterwards. It is wise to assure people that comments are not being made about them and that the notes will be available for people to see. The note-taker is performing a service for the group: the notes are to help the facilitator and group recall the points made.

9. **Aids and blocks to communication**

A multitude of books and articles have been written about both verbal and non-verbal communication. For our purposes this section is limited to indicating areas which could well be reflected on and explored by facilitators.

Listening

The quality of your listening enhances both the participation of those to whom you are listening and your ability to identify key factors in what is being said. The skill of listening is acquired by practice. Three important aspects of listening are discussed separately below:

(a) *Being present to others*

Reflecting on what you experience when someone does not pay full attention to you, can be instructive. I remember talking to a Salvation Army officer at a gathering of national youth workers. He remarked on the fact that most people seemed to be paying more attention to who else they might meet than to the person with whom they were conversing. He seemed to have read my mind and I felt chastened: although never fully learnt, that lesson has never left me. Part of Zen[2] is the art of being present with one's whole being to what one is doing: conscious concentration. Developing this skill starts with considering how you pay attention. What helps you to do so? What distracts you? What can you learn from the way others do or do not pay attention to you? It can be salutary to remind oneself that it is particularly necessary to listen not only to those with whom you agree, but to others from whom you differ.

(b) *Hearing what is not being said*

People communicate through their clothes, the tone and pitch of their voice, what they are actually saying and what they are not saying. Much of this communicates itself to us at a sub- or semi-conscious level. It is valuable to focus on these different elements in order to become more sensitive to the full range of ways in which a person or group is communicating with us.

Speculate about people you see in trains or walking down the street: you are unlikely ever to verify your speculations but you will increase the alertness of your observation. Non-verbal communication from the point of view of what the facilitator communicates is considered on page 110.

(c) *Really understanding and showing you understand*

As you listen you are reflecting, putting things together, trying to make sense both of what is being said and what is communicated in other ways, testing out your hunches to help you to understand what is going on.

You show people that you understand them by your questions as you check that you have heard them correctly, and by your comments and responses which tell them you are taking their ideas and feelings seriously. Interrupting with a comment which appears to ignore what they have said tells them the opposite.

Listen to yourself while you listen to others: this may seem a contradiction but it is an effort to bring into consciousness what is being communicated at a deeper level. It can be particularly helpful when you are stuck and do not know how to respond. Becoming aware of what is going on within *you* at this point can give you an insight into a helpful way of responding.

Despite all that has been said, for the good of the group it may at times be necessary to interrupt a person (p. 139).

Good listening is catching. The way you listen will influence others. However, you may wish to develop the listening skills of a group in some way. You could raise the question in discussion, possibly using the three points above or you may want to try out some listening exercises. Many of these will be found in Gerard Egan's book *You and Me*[3] and in other books on communicating skills[4].

Differing wavelengths

The difficulty of understanding people sufficiently to feel relaxed and able to have a useful or rewarding exchange of thoughts and feelings can be felt acutely if you are working in an alien culture or with people of a different discipline. People may use coded language[5] or have a different conceptual framework. You may feel you are out of your intellectual or academic depth or simply be unable to follow an accent to which your ear is unattuned. This can be debilitating and inhibit your skills as a facilitator.

The effect can be so paralysing one cannot 'hear' what is being said or take in things one would normally understand. The danger at such times is to disparage oneself: "I'm stupid, ignorant, out of my depth . . ." or to disparage them: "they're too high falutin', theoretical, use jargon" or to become silent, either backing away from the conversation or pretending to follow it, hoping that something will be said which makes sense of the discussion. The likelihood is that one gets further and further out of one's depth and anxiety increases in case people try to elicit some response from you.

When struggling with this problem I have found the following suggestions helpful, some when the problem is minor, others when it is acute:

- Use a variety of ways to indicate you do not understand: ask questions; ask people to repeat what they are saying in different words; summarise what you think they are saying and ask them if you have grasped their meaning; ask someone else to clarify what is being said; ask them to put what they are saying in terms a lay person can understand. If the person or group is concerned to be properly understood they will welcome such questions as an indication of your interest. Explain "I am asking you because I want to understand."

- Be open with them: "I'm finding it hard to understand or grasp the full meaning of what you're saying." Ask if they face the difficulty of not being understood by some people. Do they find other people sympathetic to their ideas? Say, "Can you help me to grasp what you are saying?" Most people like to be asked for help.

- Suggest they tell their story, describing how they came across these ideas, the effect on them, on other people, on their work, and why the ideas are so important to them now.

- Admit you are not following the details of their argument: "It may not be necessary to do so, but can you put clearly your main point which bears on the topic?" "What do you see to be the particular significance of these ideas?" "Why are you saying this now?"

- Ask them to write something for you, recommend something you can read on the subject, and/or ask if they or someone else would talk to you about it outside the group.

- Suggest some work is done in sub-groups. Take the opportunity to clarify what you don't understand and to decide what you can do. Talk to your co-worker about the problems you are facing.

One result of experiencing this difficulty and working your way through it, is to increase awareness of what other people may be feeling in a group in which they are strangers, not understanding all that is being said, and feeling nervous and inhibited as a result. It may also make you question how much you really understand those whom you think you know. The painful experience, and time and effort demanded in overcoming it, can increase your sensitivity.

Conflicting Expectations

If it becomes clear during the meeting that different expectations are leading to confusion or conflict or are inhibiting participation, take time to clarify what is at issue and work towards some agreement about the best way to proceed (p. 78). Problems which are swept aside rather than tackled are likely to fester and prove difficult to handle later on. Problems ignored rarely go away.

The use of our five senses

Everyone has a preferred sense through which what they experience is most vividly communicated. It can be helpful to remember this when talking with a group so that you use the different senses. For instance, checking out that you are communicating can be done in a number of ways: Can you *see* what I'm getting at? Can you *grasp* this? Are you *hearing* me? Does this make sense to you? Am I communicating? Are you with me? Do you get *the feel* of this? Does it *ring* a bell? Do you *see* the point? *Magic Demystified*[5] by Lewis and Pucelik is a fascinating book on this topic – and on many others.

Diagrams and models

The value and use of various kinds of diagrams and developing one's skill have already been discussed on pages 66 and 98.

Jargon

This is the use of words or phrases developed to communicate within specific groups or spheres of work and which are often not understood or misunderstood by those outside, whether it is academic jargon, or the 'abbreviated code'[6] used in a family or street gang. Using basic English and encouraging others to do so ensures that everyone is more likely to be included rather than excluded. It also encourages clarity of thought. Jargon may be meaningful when used or created by a group at a particular time but its meaning can become dulled by time and if used in a record of a meeting it needs explanation.

Emotive language and stereotypes

Some words arouse strong feelings and their use can make it more difficult to think objectively about the topic under discussion. For example, some generally emotive words are 'hooligans' and 'highbrows'. According to the group other words may be positively or negatively emotive, for example, 'fundamentalist', 'right' or 'left'. Clearly the use of emotive words cannot always be avoided but it is worth questioning whether a more objective word would promote a more rational discussion. Using stereotypes can discourage exploratory thought.

The use of imagery, metaphor, and symbols

An area which would repay further study is the use in groups of imagery such as metaphors or symbols in providing creative thought and new insights. Gareth Morgan uses metaphors to stimulate new thinking in his book on organisations.[7] He talks of a metaphor as "a way of thinking and a way of seeing that pervades how we understand our world." He goes on to describe organisations in terms of machines, living organisms, brains, cultures, psychiatric prisons and so on. The way managers view their organisations influence such things as how mechanistic, bureaucratic or flexible they are, and their stress on the human aspects, information processing or the ideological aspects of organisations. Symbols also stimulate our imagination so we come to a deeper understanding or further vision of some reality.[8]

The use of imagery in this way touches chords other than the purely rational. They rouse one's emotions, evoke something deep within us and illuminate in unexpected ways. They can be useful in introducing a discussion or in subgroup work. Members of one group asked to think in this way described their organisation in terms of a windmill: it was very lively but a lot of the movement was going round in circles; with every wind, it turned to face in a different direction, yet it remained rooted to the spot. This led them to question whether the organisation was using its energy and resources to best effect.

Non-verbal communication

As facilitator you communicate something about your attitude and frame of mind before ever you open your mouth. Awareness of this naturally leads to questions such as: What am I communicating by:

- the clothes I wear and the way I wear them? Are they saying something about me or about my attitude towards the group or the occasion?

- the way I hold my body? Reflect on the difference between leaning forward or being 'laid back', being relaxed or tense, and on controlled or fidgety movements.

- my gestures? Are they likely to reinforce or distract from what I am saying? Have I acquired tiresome mannerisms?

- my eyes? Do they look beyond a person or above the group or wander to the window or bookshelf? Do I look people in the eye in a challenging or in a supportive way?

What dangers are there for me? What do I not want to communicate? What do I want to communicate? How can I best do so?

Reading about non-verbal communication can alert one to its importance. A useful book (despite its sexist title) is *Manwatching* by Desmond Morris.[9] Receiving non-verbal signals is discussed on page 106.

10. Summarising and conceptualising

Summarising and conceptualising are about amalgamating and making connections between ideas, linking disparate points together, categorising and classifying, putting shape into a mass of ideas, seeing emerging patterns under-lying the discussion. It is a complex activity yet one we automatically employ every day of our lives as we make sense of our experience.

Making a summary of a discussion or conceptualising the ideas in some way can be of enormous benefit in a group. Among other things it can:

–   help the members to re-focus on the purpose of the meeting and/or the original topic;

–   catch up anyone who has lagged behind in the thinking and be a useful check that everyone is at the same level of understanding or agreement;

–   highlight the main points or key issues from a wealth of detail and pro-vide an opportunity to re-consider ideas or suggestions;

–   move a discussion on to the next stage or overcome an impasse by clarify-ing what next needs to be thought about, and it can lead to an agreed struc-ture for the next phase of the discussion;

–   give a breather by altering the pace;

–   help people to see what progress has been made and remind people of what still remains to be done in the time available. It is always useful to summarise when drawing a meeting to a close (p. 116).

Summaries can be of various kinds: verbal or written, diagrammatic or charted, or a combination. They can be made by the facilitator, a group member or the group as a whole. However and whenever they are made, it is important to ensure all views are represented fairly and not to omit points with which you do not agree. It is also necessary to be tentative and to check your summary for accuracy and agreement if the full benefit is to be experienced. A 'bad' summary or one which some do not accept provides a poor basis for co-operative thinking. As with all worthwhile activities there are dangers and pitfalls: distorting an argument or ideas, omitting important points, swamp-ing with detail or mis-timing your summary so it interrupts the flow of discussion.

Some ways of developing the art of summarising are listed below:

•   Jot down key points as the discussion proceeds: just listing these provides a sequential summary.

•   Ask yourself, "What stands out for me? What strikes me?" Look at things from different angles.

•   Using a pad horizontally, group ideas together as they emerge and make connecting lines between them. You may find yourself shaping and reshaping, crossing out and amalgamating as you do this.

- Tell the group what you aim to do: "I want to try to span all we've talked about. I'm not sure if it will come out all right, but can I have a go?" "The discussion has gone all over the place, do you mind if I try to sort it out on the board or paper?"

- Put the main points on board or paper as they appear.

- Ask the group to make a summary together: people rarely forget the points they have contributed! You could suggest people pause and jot down the two or three key ideas from their point of view.

- Put the ideas together in diagrammatic form (p. 66).

- Ask sub-groups to hand their findings in and make a summary after the meeting which can be part of the record (p. 64).

- In writing up a record of the discussion after a meeting you are engaged in the process of summarising but doing it in peace and quiet. This is the single most helpful way in which I have developed my summarising skills (p. 123).

11. **When uncertain about how to proceed**

When overwhelmed by ideas and alternatives

The more successful you are in promoting creative participation the more likelihood there is of being overwhelmed by the sheer number of options, ideas and suggestions. It can be comforting to realise other people experience this kind of uncertainty. All real change, according to Donald Schuon, involves "passing through zones of uncertainty . . . the situation of being at sea, of being lost, of confronting more information than you can handle".[10] For example, in a YMCA in Ronsey[11] when the Secretary for the first time invited the views of members on the activities and organisation of the building and church activities, he was quite at a loss as to how to handle the enthusiastic responses he received.

This can also happen during a meeting. There are things which could help you in such a situation:

- Call a halt for a few minutes to give yourself time to think and put the ideas in some order.

- Remind yourself that you do not have to maintain control. Enlist the help of the group in summarising and clustering the ideas.

- Present the problem to the group as one which faces you all. "We've so many ideas around I'm not sure how we can handle them all. Can we think for a moment about what would be the best way to proceed?"

- Suggest you try to put some shape into the ideas after the meeting and circulate a record, or ask someone else in the group to do so (p. 123).

When you reach an impasse or your mind goes blank

This, as I know to my cost, can happen to anyone. It is useful to have ideas about what you could do. Below are a few:

- As above, give yourself – and your co-worker – time to think by suggesting people talk to their neighbour or form buzz groups to discuss a point. Or suggest a tea-break or pause for people to stretch their legs.

- If your mind goes blank or you feel stuck you could:
  - summarise the ground you have covered;
  - suggest a coffee break or a three minute 'comfort break';
  - level with the group: "My mind's gone blank. Can you help me to summarise. . . . Can you give me half a minute to check my notes. . . ." "I'm not at all sure what we should go on to. Can we think about it together?"
  - let the discussion carry on while you try to recollect yourself, and possibly take a look at your notes.

12. Intervening in a group discussion

I often experience difficulty in knowing when to intervene in a discussion and how far and when to allow the discussion to be more discursive. There can be no rules about this but thinking about questions such as those below is likely to help you decide what to do when you are in a quandary. Clearly there is little opportunity in the actual meeting to think as systematically as this!

Why should I intervene?

Some reasons are:

- to introduce the discussion;

- to encourage creative participation, for example, some of the signals which show that it can be useful or even necessary to intervene are when an individual wants to speak and cannot get a word in; when people become fidgety, restive or go to sleep; when a monologue or dialogue develops in such a way that others are excluded; when one or more start riding a hobby horse; when the atmosphere becomes tense or embarrassing; when faction breaks out; when criticism becomes destructive or someone is snubbed; when discussion turns into argument; when private conversations and whispering take place; when a person needs help to put their ideas clearly; when a mass of ideas needs to be summarised; when discussion becomes too discursive or when the original purpose of the meeting or topic seems forgotten; when information is needed; when people keep repeating themselves; when people look confused; when 'red herrings' are introduced or when anecdotes are too lengthy or off the point; when discussion has become unrealistic, too abstract or general, or moved into a 'safe' area when it should be challenging; when the facilitator wants to question the accuracy, bias or acceptability of ideas;

- to give the facilitator's contribution, for example, to put forward your own ideas for consideration, or to state your position on an issue (p. 91) or feed in information;

- to summarise the discussion (p. 110).

Deciding whether or not to intervene

The following questions may help you to decide whether or not to intervene:

- What signals can I pick up to show I need to intervene?
- What do I hope to achieve through my intervention? (Will it help a particular individual and/or the group?)
- What will happen if I *don't* intervene?
- Would it be disruptive or threatening or diminish spontaneity?
- Would it cause offence? Would it appear defensive or partisan?

How best to intervene?

Pondering the suggestions below may help to ensure that the outcome of an intervention is positive:

- Try to avoid interrupting someone or if you feel you must interrupt, do it tentatively or with an apology. A person may need to get something off their chest and be listened to.

114

- Reflect on your own experience and learn from the kind of interventions you have found helpful and those which have had a negative effect.

- Offer to summarise what is emerging from the discussion.

- Ask a question rather than make a statement: this is more likely to get people's attention and put the discussion back on course or deepen it.

13. **Responding to unexpected questions or requests**

However carefully you prepare for a meeting something unexpected can deflect you or cause things to go awry, for instance, a question or request which surprises you and to which you do not know how to reply. Basically you have three choices:

- *To answer at once.* People often expect an immediate reply and you may allow yourself to be pressurised into giving an unconsidered response which you later regret.

- *Postpone your answer.* There are various ways of doing this and at the same time indicating your goodwill and desire to take the question or request seriously. For instance:

  - Share with those concerned the predicament in which you are and your feelings of unease at giving an immediate reply. Most people will have had a similar experience and will empathise with you.

  - Use such phrases as, "I would like time to think about that one. . . . My immediate response is x, but can I come back to you when I've given it further thought? I would like to discuss that with colleagues. . . . I need to find out more information before I reply. . . . I would not do justice to your question if I answer off the cuff. . . . We do not have time to deal with that adequately in the time available. . . . That is an important question but it is going to take us right off the subject we are working on at the moment. Can we note it and deal with it later?" It is import-ant to ensure that you *do* deal with the point later.

- *To work at it with the group.* If you are being asked questions that imply that you have all the answers and you wish to avoid a 'question and answer' session or being seen as the expert, you need to find a way of getting the person or group to think about the point being raised but without putting people down and making them feel they have done the wrong thing. Get the group to engage with the question:

  - "Has anyone else faced this situation. . . ? " "What do other people think. . . ? "

- Use such phrases as "The question I would want to ask myself is . . .", "I think I would begin by exploring. . . ."
- Be open with the group: "I don't want to turn this into a question and answer session. We've all had experience. . . ."
- Clarify the question in words or diagrams and ask questions to stimulate members to think.

If a member asks a question which, for any reason, causes group members to raise their eyebrows, you need to take it seriously to save that person's face and to make all questions allowable. It can help to state at the start that there is no question which should not be asked or which is outlawed.

14. Responding to last minute criticism

At times, I have been at a loss, when about five minutes before the end of the meeting, someone raises a question or makes a statement or criticism which devalues all that has been done during the meeting. This can have a devastating effect on you and the group and produce a tense or uneasy atmosphere. There is no panacea but you could:

- explore and clarify the criticism, if you can in the time available;
- ask the rest of the group what they think about what X is saying, but they may be so taken aback they do not respond adequately and the implication of having wasted the time remains; or they may be afraid to take X on;
- disagree as courteously as possible (you do not want to end on an argument) and re-summarise. If you can admit to or agree with any of the criticism, it is not only more honest but you are more likely to be able to draw out the implications of the criticism so you end on a positive note;
- ask people if they wish to extend the meeting to deal with the points raised or suggest dealing with them at another time, or ask a few people stay on to work through them and say notes of the discussion will be included in the record.

III. CONCLUDING A MEETING

The conclusion of a meeting can be crucial in determining its outcome. From a 'good' ending people will go away with feelings of satisfaction and stimulation, things to think about or do, and look forward to future meetings. On the other hand, a 'bad' ending can deflate and depress people, leave them angry, alienated or apathetic and make it more difficult to promote participation of a creative kind in future.

1. **Timing**

More emphasis is often placed on beginning meetings on time than ending them on time. It is important to try and honour time boundaries although it may become clear that it is right to extend them and necessary to negotiate a further 'few minutes' or 'another half hour'. To be doctrinaire and close at a creative moment or when a decision is about to be reached would be dysfunctional. Members need to be involved in deciding what to do if time runs out.

Other alternatives are to set up a special meeting, postpone items until next time, or ask a small group to deal with urgent issues.

On the other hand, a meeting may finish its work before the time specified. It is better to close early than to mark time. The facilitator could ask the group what it wishes to do with the time: Stop early? Open up another topic? Socialise?

2. **Concluding the business**

If you have made a 'concluding check list' now is the time to use it (p. 55).

It can be useful to bring the meeting to a conclusion by tentatively summarising in a positive way what the meeting has been about: what has been achieved, what has not been achieved, what still remains to be done, and what the next steps might be, in order to come to a common mind about the future.

In doing this, it may be helpful to refer to the process. For example, "We all got very excited by x" or "We had to struggle to find our way through y", "It took a lot of effort and concentration, and at times we flagged." It helps a group if more difficult moments can be acknowledged openly: "We got quite heated about some points but we worked through them," or "We've decided to discuss them later when we've had time to reflect and cool down." If the meeting appears to have been unsatisfactory or even something of a disaster, it is best to say so as honestly as possible while raising hopes for the future. For example, "I am feeling uneasy about the way the meeting has gone and maybe some of you are?" or "Possibly we all need to go away and think about it. We seem to have raised more questions than answers and I detect a bit of frustration around. It is so complex that I feel we need to do some more work to try and sort it out, so we can get off to a good start when we next meet. What do you think?"

When a group has not made as much headway as it hoped, rather than say, "We couldn't decide about this" try considering it positively, "We thought long and hard about this and although we have not got to the stage of being able to decide, we've turned over the ground, we've still agreed it is something we must work through together. We have a lot we now need to think about" It can also be useful to be quite specific about what people could well reflect on and possibly discuss informally before the next meeting.

When the business of the meeting has not been finished, it may be useful to ask an individual, or a sub-group, to do some further thinking or exploration to bring to the next meeting, or the facilitator may decide to do this.

3. **Preparing for the next meeting** (p. 78)

Members may be asked to do some thinking or reading, or there may be some tasks to be carried out or information to be sought. It may be useful to make contingency arrangements in case difficulties arise: to arrive at the next meeting only to find that the work has not been done or done inadequately can cause frustration and a loss of morale. It is important to ensure that people are being realistic about the tasks they take on in terms of the time and possibly the expertise needed. Only thus will the next round of discussion be likely to make good headway.

4. **The record**

The note-taker and the group need to be clear about what will happen to the notes and who is producing a record of the meeting: the note-taker or the facilitator or both together? When will it be circulated? If the record will take some time it can be useful to circulate an immediate 'action sheet', noting who has undertaken to do what and by when, together with the date of the next meeting. The difference between minutes and a structured record is outlined on page 77. Briefing note-takers is described on page 104. The writing of a structured record is considered on page 123.

5. **Assessing a meeting**

Various ways of engaging members in an assessment of a meeting are considered in Part Seven under 'Encouraging good practice in others' (p. 186). On some occasions it may be useful to spend a brief time reflecting together at the end of a meeting with some general questions such as:

How do you feel we've done?
What have we achieved tonight?
What do you think about the meeting?
What have you found helpful about it?
What was unhelpful about it?
What improvements could we make in the way we run future meetings?

Assessing a meeting on your own or with a co-worker is discussed on pages 126 and 131.

6. Ending a meeting

The appropriate ending of a meeting depends very much on the kind of meeting it is. It can be important to thank people and express appreciation for their contributions or even 'for sticking with it' when a meeting has been difficult. It can leave a bad feeling if the facilitator appears over-anxious to depart once the meeting is finished or abruptly rushes off. If time allows, a more leisurely ending can build relationships. Some groups like to end with a few minutes of quiet together, or have a drink and socialise.

CHECK LIST FOR USE AT THE END OF A MEETING (p. 55)

Who will take action on what? Are we all clear and agreed?

Are we all clear and agreed about what decisions have been recorded and what still remains to be done?

Is any contact necessary with absentees: when? what? by whom?

Are arrangements for writing and circulating the record in order?

Have we made arrangements for future meetings: dates, times, venues, subject matter, etc.?

Do we need to clear anything for confidentiality? Is there anything which should be omitted from the record?

---

1. See Ref. 25 p. 82.
2. Zen, the Japanese version of Ch'an sect of Buddhism in China, is noted for its simple austerity, its mysticism leading to personal tranquillity, and its encouragement of education and art (*Fontana Dictionary of Modern Thought,* p. 682).
3. Gerard Egan, *You and Me: the Skills of Communicating and Relating to Others* (Brooks Cole Publishing Co. USA 1977).
4. Pat Petrie, *Communicating the Kingdom: Communication skills for Christians* (A Grail Publication 1992). Esther Gordon, *Wholetime: A Handbook for Workshops* (Grail Publications 1996).
5. Basil Bernstein, *Class, Codes and Control* (Paladin 1971).
6. Byron A. Lewis and Frank Pucelik, *Magic Demystified, A Pragmatic Guide to Communication Change* (Metamorphous Press 1982).
7. Gareth Morgan, *Images of Organisations* (Sage Publications 1986), p. 12.
8. F.W. Dillistone, *The Power of Symbols* (SCM Press 1986), p. 13.
9. Desmond Morris, *Manwatching, A Field Guide to Human Behaviour* (Jonathan Cape 1977).
10. Donald Schuon, *Beyond the Stable State,* Reith Lecture (BBC 1971).
11. This example is more fully described in Lovell and Widdicombe *op.cit.* p. 115, Note 15, p. 82.

PART FOUR

After and between meetings

At best, meetings not only result in some definite outcome in terms of decisions to be implemented but also make for the well-being of the team, community or group. What happens after a meeting may or may not contribute to both these ends. Where a meeting has been unsatisfactory on either or both counts, any negative effects can often be overcome or ameliorated subsequently by the facilitator. This section focuses on using the time after and between meetings in order to maximise the good and minimise any harmful effects. It is as necessary, therefore, to set time aside after a meeting as it is to take time to prepare for it.

1. **Writing a structured record** (p. 77)

Circulating a record or minutes to members can enhance the value both of the meeting itself and subsequent ones and is often necessary if decisions taken are to be implemented (p. 167). The writing of minutes is a fairly common skill and excellent books are available on it.[1] The writing of immediately available notes has been described on page 104. The writing of a record, that is, structuring the basic notes into a potentially useful account as a means of promoting development of the group, corporately and individually, is a more difficult skill.

It is a task which may be done by the recorder or the facilitator. My own experience is that doing this task can be a useful method of self training: it not only helps you to see the key points which have emerged in the discussion but it develops a facility to spot crucial points while a discussion is actually taking place and thus to order and shape things in your own mind. Thus you become more skilled in introducing structure into a discussion in a way which helps people to contribute creatively.

Working on the record soon after the meeting increases the likelihood that the accuracy of your impressions and your memory will help you judge the significance of points made, but a lapse of time is also necessary in order to assimilate all that has been said and for the necessary coherence to develop.

The objective in writing a record is so to order the material that the sequence and pattern emerge and that considerations which contributed to reaching certain conclusions and the decisions and responsibilities for implementing and reviewing them are clear.

In order to do this, it may be helpful to:
–   overview all the notes and get out the categories or sections;

- formulate headings so they describe accurately what is to follow and put them in order;
- sort out the points under each heading: you will be changing the order of the contributions as you do this;
- put 'action' in the margin followed by the initial of the person(s) concerned;
- avoid including people's names as a general rule: it can be embarrassing for people who spoke much or little or who find a view attributed to them long after they have moved away from it.

Checking the record: Do this with the group at the following meeting or ask for comments through the post. This is an important part of the process. It ensures that you have not significantly distorted the meaning or omitted important points. Such a record is then owned by the group who can use it to refer to or to build on. It is worth keeping basic notes in case differences of opinion or confusion arise or anything needs checking out.

CHECK LIST AFTER WRITING A RECORD

Have I described accurately what happened? Have I included:
- all the significant points made?
- any relevant note about the general atmosphere of the meeting?
- the decisions made?
- the action to be taken? Do I need to note the person responsible for taking action or produce an action sheet?
- the time and place of the next meeting(s)?

Could it be misleading or cause offence?

Is it necessary to include everything?

Do any papers or information need to be circulated with the record?

Does it need an accompanying note to any member or to any absentee?

Would it help, for later reference, to number the paragraphs or give the record a reference number?

---

2. Maintaining the well-being of the members

Meetings are prime opportunities to build up *esprit de corps* in a group, community or team. Taking time to reflect on how people related to each other and to the group as a whole can be useful. Ask yourself:

- What do I feel about the way the group as a whole operated? What was good/less good about it?

- Do I feel uneasy about anyone or the way they did or did not participate?

- Are there any misunderstandings which could be cleared up and if so would it be best done by a visit, casual meeting, phone call or letter?

- Did I react or speak to anyone in a way which I now see to be clumsy or hurtful? If so, do I need to take any action to restore the relationship or dispel any negative feelings?

- Do I have to check or inform any absentees about provisional or definite dates for future meetings, decisions made, or catch them up in any way? (p. 79). Absent members who are ignored are liable to lose interest. If the group is working on matters of central importance affecting the lives of all concerned, the utmost care needs to be taken to ensure that people who do not attend a meeting are kept in touch so that they can subsequently participate as fully as possible.

3. **Implementing decisions**

The implementation of major decisions is considered on page 167. The questions below are more immediate ones which the facilitator would do well to consider after a meeting.

- Are all concerned clear about their tasks and able to get on with them?

- What have I undertaken to do? When and how am I going to do it?

- Does anything need to be done at this stage about any decisions or matters held over for a future meeting or in relation to any unachieved objective?

- Do I need to make any notes as an *aide memoire* for myself?

- Do I need to put any dates in my diary?

- Am I uneasy about any of the decisions or proposed action?

- What makes me uneasy: the way it was decided? the suggested way of tackling the task? Do I feel the task is necessary or appropriate? Is the timing right? Is there anything I can do about this? Should I write or speak to anyone?

When working with a group to which I do not belong, I have had qualms afterwards about some aspects of the event. I have found it useful to make contact, either in conversation or in writing, and say that "I have been reflecting on what we did together, and feel uneasy about x" As an outside facilitator, my responsibility only ends after I have done my own assessment of the work and done my best to rectify any major shortcomings.

4. **Assessing and learning from meetings**

Much significant learning is likely to take place through reflecting on meetings shortly after them (p. 187). This constitutes self-training and promotes development of one's skills. The discipline of a systematic and thorough evaluation after key meetings will encourage a habit of less vigorous assessment on other occasions. Spending even a brief period writing down your general thoughts and feelings shortly after a meeting often enables you to capture some things which would later elude you.

Reflecting on a meeting can have positive or negative effects. If it seems to have gone well, whilst it may be a boost to your morale and encourage you to work even more thoroughly, you might be tempted to rest on your laurels. A meeting which appears to have been a disaster can deflate, depress and disable you but it might also challenge you to redoubled efforts. To increase your objectivity you may find it helpful to write things down or to think things through with a colleague who may or may not have been present, but who will respond in an objective, non-judgmental and supportive way while exploring thoroughly the inherent challenge of the situation and the implications in terms of future practice. Assessing and learning from a meeting with a co-worker is considered on page 131.

From what has been said above, it is clear that while assessing a meeting may be an invigorating and enjoyable exercise, it can also be painful and disturbing. Here too a colleague can help you to work through any negative feelings as they affect you and potentially other people inside or outside the group (p. 42).

The different aspects suggested below are complexly interrelated. The questions may help you to think systematically and in the round. Select and amend those most appropriate to you and your situation. Why not start by thinking about one or two aspects or parts of the meeting rather than by working your way through them all?

My feelings

What are my overall feelings: – about the meeting?
                                – about my part in it?

What makes me feel like this?
How do I think others felt?
Have I any niggles or a sense of unease?
Was I nervous or afraid at any particular moment? If so, what caused it?
How could I have coped better?

What was achieved? (p. 46)

How far did I achieve my objectives or help the group achieve theirs?
Was there any lack of achievement due to unrealistic or inappropriate objectives or due to my lack of skill or . . . ?
Did I or we achieve other things?
How do I feel about this?

My performance (p. 85)

Did the meeting get off to a good start? What was helpful or unhelpful about the way I introduced the meeting? How could it have been improved?
Did things flag or did the momentum keep up or increase? How was this affected by anything I did?
How did the meeting end? Could I have ended it better? In what way?
Is there anything I can do about this now?
What did I do particularly well/badly?
Were the questions searching enough (p. 56)?
Were the tasks we worked on appropriate?
Did I raise the necessary questions, even if they were hard or challenging?
How did I respond to anything which particularly surprised me (p. 115)?

Members' participation (p. 135)

Think about each member in turn:
  – how much did they take part?
  – how did they discuss? contribute? listen?
  – how open were they?
  – how did they respond to each other and to me?

What did I do or not do which affected their participation?
How far did I create an atmosphere in which all felt free to speak?
What problems did I face? What did I do about them and with what result?
What else could I have done?

The task of the meeting

Were members clear about the objective of the meeting and about what they were discussing and deciding (p. 44-46)?
Had they come prepared? If not, how could I have ensured they had prepared better (p. 78)?
Had I prepared adequately? Could I have prepared better in any way (p. 35)?
How far was the way I structured the meeting helpful (p. 49)? In what ways could it have been improved? Was I sufficiently flexible (p. 90)?
Did I get all points of view considered?
Was I realistic in terms of time (p. 77)?
Were there any other factors which helped or hindered the meeting? (e.g. venue? time? size? sub-group work? use of diagrams or flip chart?) (p. 80)
What could I have done to avoid or ameliorate any unhelpful factors?

Key learning

Are there any general learning points about working with people which I can identify and apply to future meetings? Listing these will enable you to build up your own code of good practice.

6. Coping with failure

Few if any of us do not feel at times that we have had a disastrous and frustrating meeting or been unable to help a group make or implement decisions. Such 'failures' hold enormous learning potential provided we are prepared to spend the time and emotional energy involved in facing them.

The following questions were found useful by two leaders of a voluntary organisation who discussed 'Coping with failure'.

What do I find most difficult when faced with failure?

They listed things such as a sense of inadequacy, self-blame, lost opportunity, self-doubt and despair.

What are the feelings this arouses in me?

They came up with four dominant feelings: insecurity, depression, disappointment, fear of rejection.

What would help me to control my emotions and use them constructively?

They were surprised at the length of their list compared to the lists above. They included things varying from "share with a trusted friend" and "accept we all make mistakes" to "see it in context and long term" and "remind myself of original purpose".

What can I learn from this?

- Value myself: this helps me to be less defensive.
- Use negative experiences to get in touch with my emotions.
- See failure as a growth point and discuss it from this angle.
- Focus on the things I can do and have some control over.
- Review my internal, in-built attitudes.

In relation to a specific 'incident' or 'failure' it can be useful to work through it systematically. For instance, with a group, I examined a weekend conference which was something of a failure, in order to see exactly what it was in the publicity, preparation, introduction, conduct and ending which could have led to the unsatisfactory conclusion. We learnt much from this for future planning. It can be equally useful, half-way through a series of meetings which are not going well, to examine what is happening and identify what changes you need to make to improve subsequent meetings.

Writing out the incident and working through it as a case study, according to a structured method developed by Avec[2] based on the work of T.R. Batten,[3] can be salutary and enable you not only to learn what you might have done to avoid or ameliorate the problem but how to redeem the situation. It can also have a major effect on your feelings. Case studies can be used by an individual as described below or by a group.

A case is a description of a specific instance in which you did not achieve what you set out to achieve. It briefly describes your objective, your initial assessment of the situation, what you tried to do and exactly how you tried to do it, and with what effect. Studying a case involves identifying the underlying problem, systematically diagnosing its causes and determining specific and general implications.

This is often therapeutic and cathartic: it objectifies a problematic situation which is often charged with feelings of frustration and guilt. It is generally best to write in the first person "I was planning x". Start off by describing what you were trying to achieve. Then, in relation to the key events, describe the essence of the things you did in the order in which you did them and what others did in response. The case should end with a statement of the dissatisfaction and problems with which the case culminated. The case can be about something which is of current concern or it can be about something that is no longer an issue but was never satisfactorily resolved, evaluated, or worked through. It should be as brief as you can make it whilst providing all the relevant information clearly.

No incident can be too small to form the basis of a case. Big things hinge on apparently small events in human affairs.

The basic structure of the case study, therefore, could be something like this:

- the initial situation and your objective;
- the key events in the order in which they occurred, your actions and the significant responses made by others;
- an assessment of the final situation and your dilemma, concerns or the problems facing you.

The method consists of the following stages:

(a) Write out the case.

(b) Diagnose possible reasons for your 'failure', specifically in terms of what you did or did not do which contributed to the unsatisfactory nature of the end result.

(c) Assess what is 'going for' you in the situation: in determining any future action, one needs to take into account both the negative and positive aspects of the situation.

(d) Determine the implications. This may be done:

- by working out in specific detail just what you could have done in the initial situation, or at any selected point in the story, to avoid the mistakes which led to the failure; or
- by working out just what you should do now to redeem the situation in the light of (b) and (c) above.

(e) Draw out any general implications or conclusions in terms of insights into principles underlying effective development work with people.

This may appear to be a painstaking exercise but it is one I recommend, having experienced its beneficial effects on my work. At first, it took me a couple of hours but now I am able to move through the steps far more quickly when time is at a premium.

7. **The co-worker's job** (p. 61)

The co-worker may help with any of the above tasks. What role the co-worker performs after a meeting will vary according to circumstances and what you agree between you in relation to the areas discussed above.

The record: Could the co-worker write up the record, or check it for accuracy, clarity and completeness, or read it for acceptability standing in the shoes of the members (p. 123)?

Maintaining the well-being of the members (p. 124) and *Implementing decisions* (p. 167): In relation to both areas a co-worker is likely to see things differently, and may pick up points you miss.

Assessing and learning from the meeting: The co-worker's comments and observations written independently immediately after a meeting will be useful in subsequent discussions about how it went. You may wish to improve your skills by asking your co-worker to note specific instances of good or bad practice, when the group responded well or reacted negatively, and anything else from which you could subsequently learn. Assessing and learning from meetings is discussed in greater detail on page 126.

NOTES

1. *The Write Stuff: Effective Minutes and Agendas* by Geraldine Sayers Cowper (The Industrial Society Press 1991).
2. Avec was a Service Agency for Church and Community Work, from 1976 to 1994 of which I was Co-Director from 1976 to 1992. It was an Associated Institution of Roehampton Institute and a registered charity. A critical account of what made and marred this institution is to be found in Lovell, George, *Avec: Agency and Approach* (An Avec publication 1996).
3. See four books by T.R. Batten, *Training for Community Development: A Critical Study of Method* (O.U.P. 1965), pp. 39-40 and 113-120; and *The Non-Directive Approach in Group and Community Work* (O.U.P. 1967); pp. 96-100. *The Human Factor in Community Work* (O.U.P. 1965) and *The Human Factor in Youth Work* (O.U.P. 1970) contain examples of actual cases and discussion of them by a group.

PART FIVE

Facing common situations and problems

A facilitator needs to be prepared to take effective action when problems arise.

It has already been said that problems are obstacles we face as we strive to achieve things which are inherently difficult. No one can be secure against facing new problems or difficult situations. Working at them is demanding and challenging but can be satisfying and rewarding. The problem-tackling sequence outlined on page 74 can be a useful tool to help one do so.

Some common situations and problems are explored below: the list cannot be comprehensive, neither can the suggestions for tackling them. The intention here is simply to give some hints and ideas both to engender a hopeful realisation that there is usually something which can be done to ameliorate or avoid a problem, and to encourage creative thinking about how to do so.

The hardest part of thinking is to find the questions which will motivate us and which are likely to expose the core issue. Therefore many questions are suggested in the sections below. Where appropriate they are divided into what you could do before, during and after a meeting. Choose those questions and suggestions which appeal to you. Enlist the services of a co-worker if you have one.

1. **A lack of participation**

You may be faced at different times with one or more people who for a variety of reasons and in various ways do not participate in the meeting. You may think of them as silent, apathetic or dependent, you may suspect them of being lazy or lacking in self confidence. Your surmises may or may not be accurate. Being silent, of itself, does not necessarily mean a member is not participating: she may be naturally quiet and agree with what is being said or be weighing things up before speaking.[1]

Before a meeting

- Describe as accurately as you can what non-participants do or do not do in a meeting. Do they behave in the same way at every meeting whatever the task or topic? What are they like before or after meetings, and on other occasions? Is it only when *you* are leading the discussion or when X or Y is present or absent?

- Diagnose why you think they act in this way. For instance, is it lack of self confidence, a habit of laziness? Are they less able or intelligent, slower than other members? Are they afraid of making a mistake or appearing silly or ignorant? Can they understand? Are they over-stretched, daunted by the task or tired? Have they been discouraged by a bad experience or been hurt in the past? Are they present under pressure, tired or uninterested in the subject? Could they be preoccupied, upset or living in a world of their own? Do other people ignore or ostracise them or snub them in any way? Do they feel the task or meeting is irrelevant or will fail? Is there jealousy or conflict between people?

- Reflect on the occasions when you are silent. Does this throw any light on the situation?

- Have an exploration and non-judgmental discussion with them as to why they do not participate and what might help them to do so.

- Ensure, especially when dealing with apathy, that any task the group attempts is likely to have a satisfactory solution: apathy feeds on failure.

- Identify any times when they have participated, or shown interest. Explore why you think it was so and read off the implications.

At the meeting

Whether the suggestions below are useful will depend very much on the reasons for the lack of participation. Many of the ideas are put forward in other parts of this book but for easy reference they are grouped here. Those more appropriate when one or two members are quiet are followed by those more appropriate when there is a lack of participation from the group as a whole.

When one or two members do not participate:

- Stress at the start of the meeting the value in each person's contribution: each is unique, with different experiences, views, ideas, etc.

- Listen and make something of all that is said and encourage others to do the same. Affirm small ideas.

- Ask questions which give people a chance to respond; for example, "Anyone want to add anything?" or "Does anyone who has not yet said anything, want to. . . ?"

- Avoid putting them on the spot, "John, what do you think about this?" as that can be counter productive and embarrass them.

- Try to catch their eye, silently inviting them to contribute.

- Ensure any points they have contributed are included in the record.

- Raise questions to get people thinking about the suggestions and ideas, especially your own. For example, "I'm saying this, but I'm not at all sure I'm right or that it would work, can we look at it critically. . . ?" Work on the pros and cons, or possible good and bad side effects of various proposals.

- Make time for people to jot down their own ideas before inviting discussion.

- Make use of buzz groups, sub-groups and working in pairs: many people are able to talk in smaller groups (p. 61).

- Ensure that the people want to be at the meeting (p. 139) and want to discuss the topic (p. 88).

- Discover what motivates people and build on that.

- As appropriate go gently or be forthright: do not put undue pressure on people but remember some pressure may be necessary to help them to enter into things.

When the group as a whole does not participate:

- *Have a sharing and listening exercise*. With people who have never been used to meetings and discussions it can be useful, as a starter, to have a series of small group meetings in which people have prepared something they can share; for example, a passage from scripture or a book they've read; and why they have chosen it. There is no discussion; each contribution is listened to in turn. This gives people an opportunity to hear their own voice and to be listened to by others and can gradually build up confidence in having something to say which is worth listening to. A few words on the necessity to listen and to show you are listening could well introduce this (p. 105).

- *Have a discussion about participation*: For example, as outlined on page 189, ask people to jot down one or two things which help them and one or two things which hinder them from participating. Share these and build up a 'code of good practice' or some 'ground rules' together.

- *Consider energy flow*. With a group which appears tired and apathetic, especially if it seems to have 'gone flat' in an uncustomary way, it could be useful to have a discussion about energy flow. John Sandford has pointed out that human beings – and therefore groups – can only conserve energy for a limited time and that energy flow in and out is necessary for human and spiritual well-being.[2] Try plotting, as a group, when the energy level has been high and when low. What has energised us as a group in the past? Why? What has sapped our energy in the past or now? What can we now do to renew our energy as a group? (It might be useful to precede this by a discussion on energy flow in individuals.)

- *Share the problem:* Put the problem to the group and work through it using the problem tackling sequence (p. 74).

2. **Dealing with a dominant member**

This is a common and multi-faceted difficulty.

Before or between meetings

- Explore what appears to be happening in the group by asking yourself such questions as:

    - In what way does X dominate the group? Is it by talking too much or by silence?

    - Why does X behave like this? (Your answers may have to be speculative.) Is it to do with having no one to talk to, with status or expertise, natural aggressiveness, habit or the fact that no one appears to listen or take her seriously? Is she a quicker thinker, insensitive and self centred? Is she hiding a feeling of inadequacy beneath a blustery exterior, determined on a particular outcome or. . . ?

    - What is the overt effect on other members? How do they respond? Are they colluding and therefore allowing the domination to continue? Why do they respond in this way? Is it due to fear of challenging or hurting X, or a fear of breaking social ties or friendships, or a lack of awareness or belief that things could change, or a desire to keep in with X for personal advantage, or natural timidity, or lack of self confidence and, sense of inadequacy?

    - What am I doing as facilitator to exacerbate or maintain this situation? Why?

- Work on any negative feelings you may have towards the dominating person (p. 42). Ask yourself, "What might have happened in the past to make her behave like this? How might people have treated her?"

- Talk to the person concerned outside the group meeting. Establish a good relationship with her. Explain the difficulty as you see it in non-judgmental terms. For instance, rather than "You do too much talking", say something like "People seem to be relying on you to do their thinking for them", "People are not contributing their ideas".

- Enlist X as co-worker for a particular meeting: this gives you an opportunity to discuss the need for everyone to contribute and together to find ways to encourage this (p. 61).

- Think through the problem with your co-worker. Beware of forming a liaison against X. Instead, work out ways of increasing the participation of other members without snubbing the dominating person.

- Work out ways of stimulating and making opportunities for quieter people to speak (p. 135).

At the meeting

If, despite all, X starts to talk too much or dominate in other ways, you need to remain calm, courteous and accepting. You might try to intervene by:

- reassuring X that she has been heard, at the same time indicating that the contributions of other members are needed and making an opportunity for others to speak;

- laying a restraining hand on X's arm as an indicator that you want to say something. It can be useful to sit next to someone likely to be over-talkative so that your hand and body movements can at the same time be supportive of X while holding her back from over-participating;

- acknowledging her contributions "You've raised several (interesting), points": to ignore her contribution is tantamount to de-valuing her as a person;

- summarising what she has said: people may have developed a habit of not listening to her from sheer frustration and so her points never get heard;

- encouraging other people to think for themselves and participate by inviting a response to what X has said: "Can we start by considering X's first point?" or "What do other people think about what X is saying ?"

- suggesting different points of view and raising questions about all of them, including X's, thereby stimulating open and critical consideration of them and thus widening the discussion.

3. **Working with reluctant attenders**

This problem is more likely to occur in work places, colleges or residential communities where attendance is required or expected. Reluctance, whether expressed or not, can have negative effects on the atmosphere and on the facilitator. It is important to take a grip on the situation, face the problem and try to avoid or ameliorate it rather than ignore it.

Below are some things you could do. The appropriate action depends very much on the circumstances and type of meeting.

Before the meeting

- Do your best to ensure that people know what they are coming to and make as free a choice as possible to attend. This includes giving sufficient information about the time boundaries.

- Formulate the agenda with those concerned or ensure, as far as possible that it interests them and meets their needs. This may be done before or at the start of the meeting.

- When appropriate, make clear to those in authority the danger of putting undue pressure on people, and the importance of people making a free choice to attend.

At the meeting

One approach with those who are present under duress, is to try to ameliorate their reluctance, for instance, by:

- Exploring it with them: something may emerge which will enable you and them to see how the time could be made use of to their advantage.

- Helping them to come to terms with the situation: if they have to be present suggest they try to make the most of it for their own sake and that of others who want to be there.

- Getting them to take responsibility for their presence: if they belong to the organisation in which attendance at the meeting is required they have the choice between paying this cost, or, should they feel strongly enough, leaving the organisation or questioning the system and those who are pressurizing them. As facilitator I would want to ensure they face the cost of leaving or questioning the system if that is what they decide to do.

- Making the meeting as stimulating and enjoyable as possible and as short as is consonant with the work that has to be done.

4. Working with a hostile group

You may be faced with a group which is actively hostile to you and the hostility may be merited, due to a misunderstanding, or projected. Knowing or suspecting such hostility to be present to any degree allows you to prepare for it. If you have caused the hostility and particularly if it is justified, you have a more difficult task, both in dealing with your own feelings, and in working with the group to redeem the relationship.

Before a meeting

- Reflect openly and as far as you can on the possible causes of the members' hostility. Do you know what happened to make them react like this? Ask yourself if they are angry with you or whether some other cause is making them project their anger on you. Examine your own actions to see if you have unwittingly caused their anger. Maybe their anger is justified. If it is long-standing, reflect on what may be fuelling their anger.

- Explore your feelings and attitudes and decide how you will try to come to terms with the situation and control any anger you may feel towards the people concerned (p. 42). If you have caused the hostility, it can increase your objectivity to write down and work through the incident as a case study (see 'Coping with Failure' on page 128). Doing this may alert you to things you said or did which contributed to the situation. You will need to face this honestly so you can react undefensively to criticism.

- Consider the potential advantages of the situation: for instance, the people you are dealing with are energised and active; the hostility is overt and you are not working in the dark and can therefore tackle things openly; above all, there is an enormous amount which you and the group stand to learn if you are able to face and work through the situation together.

- Decide how you will respond when people criticise you or others and what you will do if people become angry at the meeting. Some ideas discussed in the section on 'Working with Conflict' may be relevant (p. 142).

At the meeting

Much will depend on the situation but a golden rule is to keep calm, undefensive and maintain a positive attitude towards the group and hold out hope of working through the difficulty. Some of the following ideas may be too risky in some situations but useful in others:

- Make an objective statement about the situation. Suggest it would be worthwhile to explore it and work through it together, and see if the group is willing to do so. Help people to say what their anger is about, take it seriously and try to see things from their point of view and discuss it without fear. Allow people to have their say, encourage them by examining what they are saying, bringing issues into the open and focusing on criticisms.

- Be prepared to acknowledge or apologise for anything you have done which has contributed to the unsatisfactory relationship. At the same time, be equally forthright about anything they may have done to exacerbate the situation. Maintain your integrity and objectivity. Do not become over-apologetic. Two parties are involved in any relationship: whichever is 'to blame', the other is not faultless. A broken relationship is not necessarily caused by malice.

- While the situation is being opened up, be alert and note for yourself any positive points which emerge, any learning points, any possible ways for-ward or ideas which may help as you work through to a solution.

- At an appropriate moment, ask if the time has now come to work out the implications of all that has been said. You may want to suggest people pause to jot down what they have learnt or any implications which strike them about anything to do or avoid "as we work together in the future". Invite those who want to do so, to share what they have written; be pre-pared to contribute your ideas. What is important is that in this part of the discussion, even though it is brief, everyone is engaged in deciding upon constructive ways of working together in the future and how to avoid or deal with any further difficulties which may arise.

- End the meeting on a positive note: express appreciation for people's open-ness and readiness to work through painful issues.

5. **Working with conflict**[3]

One effect of working non-directively is that the differences which exist among any group of people are likely to emerge. This makes for potential conflict when opposite ideas are expressed forcibly or categorically. The way in which this is dealt with can either be constructive; for instance, leading to deeper insights, more creative ideas, mutual understanding and empathy; or it can have a destructive outcome, such as worsening relationships, verbal bullying or faction.

Many books have been written ranging widely over the whole field of conflict (see the section on *Conflict* in the Bibliography). Here we are only concerned to deal with conflict which arises in meetings. Faction, when two or more sub-groups take up a definite stand in opposition to each other, is dealt with in the following section (p. 145).

When conflict appears likely:

If you suspect beforehand that conflict is likely to arise during a meeting, the following ideas may help you to prepare to deal with it constructively:

- Explore the situation, possibly by describing it on paper. What is the conflict likely to be about? Who is involved? How strongly are opposing views likely to be held? Why?

- Explore your own feelings, attitudes, behaviour and purposes in relation to it by asking yourself: What do I think and feel about it? What is my spontaneous reaction? Am I involved, implicated, partisan, or thought to be (p. 43)? How do people see me? Decide how you will deal with your feelings, especially if there is a lot of anger around or you are emotionally involved in the issue (p. 43).

- Decide on your purpose and approach. Ask yourself: What am I trying to achieve in the situation (p. 46)? How can I ensure all ideas are considered? What can I usefully say to start the meeting off (p. 86)?

Unexpected conflict:

If conflict erupts unexpectedly it may be wiser to work through it there and then or to avoid, de-fuse or try to postpone it. You may feel there is more likelihood of making matters worse if feelings are running high, time is short or you lack the needed confidence or ability. You could suggest, "I think perhaps we should give ourselves time to think or calm down rather than continue now."

Stance:

When trying to help a group tackle the conflict you need to make your position clear: that you want to help yourself and anyone else to consider and explore all ideas as openly and objectively as possible rather than argue from fixed positions. You may decide to say this or demonstrate it by the way you respond to the different contributions. Ideas on stance are developed below 'Working with faction' (p. 146).

Commitment to resolve the conflict:

I find it helpful to move the discussion away from the issue about which people are in conflict to a consideration of whether they want to try to work towards a resolution and how we might do so. At times I point out that there are two opposing views and sets of feelings, that the people concerned have very different needs and values and that a win/win rather than a win/lose solution is likely to be more satisfactory and lasting, although working for this may take time and patience. In working through the conflict, much could be learnt about resolving future conflicts, and a firm basis built for co-operation in the future.

De-personalise the issues:

Summarise the situation as objectively as possible: you will help people consider the issues clearly if you are non-judgmental and use non-emotive language. Explore with people why they differ and then ask, "How do we work at this?" Unless great hostility and rigidity is present, given goodwill, people can be very creative on such occasions (p. 99).

Working for mutual understanding:

It has been said that until you are able to argue convincingly for an opposing position, you are not able to appreciate it fully and therefore are not ready to discuss it with those concerned. There are various ways of working towards mutual understanding:

- To ensure people are really listening to and understanding each other, ask group A to explain its position to group B so that B is able to state it to A's satisfaction – and vice versa.

- Get people to stand in one another's shoes. It can be a hard struggle to get people to do this but if you succeed it can radically change attitudes (p. 74).

- Get out what people with conflicting views see as essential, and work out a compromise by 'giving and taking' on non-essentials.

- Help people in sub-groups, mixed or homogeneous, to work out a possible solution which would meet not only their own needs but those of the others (p. 61). Discussing these ideas may lead to a mutually agreeable solution.

- Affirm and re-affirm common ground – then go on to explore areas of difference. Establish what is agreed and enlarge this – and keep returning to it when differences threaten to divide. For example, the worker may say, "Five minutes ago Mr X said so and so, Miss Y is now making a similar point" or "We seem to agree about . . . ."

- Point to any responsibility the members have for the well-being of the whole group and any organisation of which the group is a part.

6. **Working with faction**[3]

Faction can result when conflict in a group has not been resolved satisfactorily and entrenched positions are taken up by two or more sets of people. What follows is by nature of 'first aid' when faction emerges in a group. Further advice or specialist expertise, especially if the problem is a long-standing one, may be needed.

Some of the points made in the preceding section on conflict apply here and are not repeated. The problem-tackling sequence may be of particular use (p. 74).

Timing

In attempting to resolve faction in a group it is worth considering the timing. Would it be best to work at it when it erupts, shortly after it has erupted, or when all is calm? Weigh the pros and cons in relation to the particular situation, taking into account:

- the emotional temperature and likely motivation to work through it;
- your own confidence and skills;
- the urgency or otherwise of the situation;
- the amount of time available both for preparation and discussion;
- the presence of the key participants.

It is important whenever you tackle it to have the commitment of those concerned, otherwise it is all too easy to exacerbate the situation. Consider too whether it would help to indicate to people in advance that you consider it could be useful to work through the difficulties between them. If you spring it on them is it likely have negative effects? If you forewarn them are they likely to prepare their defences? Is there any preparatory thinking which people could usefully do? Would some objective, non-judgmental questions get people thinking openly about the situation beforehand?

Who should deal with it?

You may or may not be in the best position to help the situation. For instance, in the example on page 67, M and N who have good relationships with both groups are in a better position than the facilitator. Ask yourself: Am I likely to be the one best able to handle it? Is there someone else who is more likely to be acceptable or effective, possibly an independent outsider? Could they help me or could I talk to them about what they might do to resolve the situation?

Stance (p. 143)

If you decide to tackle the problem yourself, consider how you want to be seen and how to get into such a position. You are more likely to be able to take constructive action to end the conflict if you are seen to be fair to both parties by saying such things as "I am not taking sides on this issue. . . . What I am wanting to do is to help you to resolve it to everyone's satisfaction. . . . There are views and feelings on both sides which we need to take seriously." This is more necessary and more difficult if you are identified with one or other party because of the colour of your skin or your denomination or views.

Towards resolution of faction

The section on 'Working with Several Groups' on page 158 may prove useful. In addition, points suggested on page 143 and the following may be helpful according to circumstances:

- In my experience I find it important to allow plenty of time for people to express themselves. They should not be encouraged to close this part of the discussion prematurely. This calls for patience. Remain calm and relaxed and show neither surprise nor shock at what people are saying. Occasionally it may help to repeat things in less emotive language or to summarise objectively.

- Get the opposing groups to note positive things about each other. It may be useful to pause occasionally to allow them to do this or to reflect on what is going on.

- Give each group time to work out what it sees to be its own strengths and weaknesses and then share these with each other.

- Make use of buzz groups periodically, especially if working with a large group.

The following method comes from work in industry by Donald G. Livingstone.[4] He suggests 'Two Rules of the Road':

- Skipper your own ship (not the other group's ship).

- Stick to what is happening now, not yesterday or tomorrow. Then go through the following steps:

    (a) Give each group 30 minutes to write down "five things the other group does which makes life more difficult for you *but* you are not to tell them what to do or how to do it".

(b) As each is making its list – ask them to spend five minutes listing (and keeping it hidden) what they think the other group will say about them.

(c) Each group shares: any comments or hints in which one group is telling the other what it should do are OUT. "Only say what they do which causes you problems." Rule (ii) says put on the list only things they are doing *now*, no raking over the past.

(d) Each group has time on its own to work out what they will do in order not to make problems for the other group.

(e) Each group shares this and it is formally accepted by the other group.

(f) Arrange a time for review.

NOTES

1. Strauss & Strauss, *op.cit.*, p. 69, Note 18 p. 82.
2. *Ministry Burnout* by John Sandford (Paulist Press 1982).
3. I am indebted to George Lovell from whom I have learnt much about dealing with conflict and faction, both through exposition, discussion, and seeing him at work with groups. In *The Human Factor in Community Work*, T.R. Batten summarises the worker's functions when dealing with faction, p. 152.
4. Donald Livingstone, "Rules of the Road", *Personnel,* January/February 1977. Donald Livingstone is Vice President, Industrial Relations, Electronics, New Jersey.

PART SIX

Specific application

Much of what has been written so far applies in many situations and to some extent to all groups. What follows is a more specific application to different types of groups and particular situations and tasks.

I GROUPS OF DIFFERENT KINDS

1. Formal groups and committees

Despite the constraints within which formal groups and committees operate, the approaches outlined in this book may be used to help their members work together in a collaborative style and to greater effect. What is written below is about ways and means of promoting participation and individual and corporate development within the more formal committee setting. It is not about effective committee structures and procedures which are already more than adequately covered in many books and pamphlets (see the section on committees in the Bibliography).

Membership.

Committees are likely to function best when members:

- have been elected or selected with care according to pre-determined criteria;
- have not been 'press-ganged' onto the committee;
- have been thoroughly briefed, and are clear about their role and function and that of the committee: they know what is expected of them and the customary procedures;
- are interested and believe in the work of the committee;
- want and have the time and ability to be active, regular and useful participants;
- collectively represent a wide range of interests, perspectives, abilities, and expertise.

In local committees it is often advisable to have a fixed period for serving, as this ensures a turnover of members with new blood and encourages more people to take an active part. Without such a procedure, a person can remain on a committee beyond the time when they usefully contribute and it can be difficult to find a courteous and tactful way of replacing them.

Forming an Agenda

An agenda may be drawn up by the chairperson or secretary, alone or together or in consultation with committee members. Such consultation is likely to ensure that the agenda consists of matters which members want to consider. Checking the agenda for acceptability at the start of the meeting can help to ensure that members are clear about it and are committed to working through it.

Some less formal committees may adopt the method of forming the agenda when they meet. This takes time, but as items are clarified so is their relative importance and the sequence in which they can best be worked through. Such an agenda-making session may be for one meeting or for a series of meetings, in which case it may need re-checking and amending at intervals.

Making the best use of time

There are various ways of making the best use of the often limited time the committee has at its disposal:

- If an agenda is to be sent out beforehand, ensure it contains sufficient information and explanation under each item and is accompanied by relevant papers, reports or background material, clearly identified, so that the actual time of the committee can be spent in clarification and discussion of the issue.

- Keep agendas to manageable length.

- Members are likely to feel more responsible for time keeping if they have had a say in establishing the timing. Note in the margin of your copy the time estimated for each item: ensure items needing longer for discussion have the necessary time. Ask for a time keeper.

- Encourage members to prepare adequately by reading records or minutes as well as agendas when they receive them rather than at the last minute.

- Check at the start of the meeting whether there is any other business: some items may fit appropriately with other items and you can assess the time they are likely to take.

- Differentiate between policy decisions in which everyone needs to have a voice and the executive action which may be thought through by a few people who are responsible for taking action.

- Identify any issues which may profit from a special meeting, due to the time needed to discuss them or the desirability of a more relaxed setting.

- Make appropriate use of working parties and sub-committees on particular issues or areas of work. Agree beforehand their terms of reference: task, area of responsibility, authority and freedom, membership, life span, procedures for reporting back and for the receiving of the report.

Introducing business

George Lovell[1] suggests that officers and members who are planning to introduce a business item to a meeting could use the following questions, to help them prepare how best to present it:

The why and the what

Why am I bringing this matter to the committee? What do I want them to do or to decide? Am I clear about the 'why' and the 'what' and the 'choices' to be made?

Information

Have I got enough information? Have they? Have I done all the work I can/must do beforehand? How can I present the point clearly and succinctly?

Time and timing

Is this the best time to raise the subject? Can this committee deal with the subject in the time? How can I save their time?

It is surprising how these approaches can become 'part of people'; how they help people to make better informed decisions; to feel in charge; and how they save time and energy.

COMMITTEE CHAIRPERSON'S CHECK LIST

- Is there any action I can take in relation to venue, arrangement of chairs and room, time or refreshments which would improve the quality of the meeting?

- What am I hoping to achieve through this meeting (my objectives) (p. 46).

- Are members likely to be clear about our structures and procedures? Do I need to check out any of them?

- How am I going to work with the committee members and get them to work with each other? What could I say at the start of the meeting to promote creative, collaborative and concentrated thinking and discussion (p. 85)?

- How am I going to ensure we keep to time (p. 77)?

- How can I/we best formulate the agenda? Is there any specific preparation needed by some or all of the members? What background information do I need to send round? When should members receive the agenda (p. 78)? How shall I deal with the AOBs?

- How can I encourage members to introduce business efficiently?

- What decisions have to be made? Would it help to agree a decision making procedure? How can I ensure we implement what we decide? Decision-making is discussed on page 161.

- Do any topics need more time, or a working party, or a special meeting? How can I help the committee to decide about this?

- Is there any way of improving the minutes?

- Do I foresee any specific difficulties and if so, is there anything I can do or ask anyone else to do beforehand, at the start or during the meeting to avoid or ameliorate them?

- How can we ensure a full turnout at a subsequent meeting? Do I need to get any dates from people whom I know are unable to be present (p. 79)?

2. **Large groups**[2]

This section is not a comprehensive guide to working with large groups. What it sets out to do is to highlight those points of crucial importance when using the approaches advocated in this book with groups of twenty and over.

The larger the group the more difficult it is to ensure active participation of all concerned and the greater the danger of people having a variety of expectations, becoming bored, misunderstanding what is being said, listening passively rather than thinking critically, and of contributions from the floor being taken less seriously than what is said from the chair.

On the other hand there is great potential for development in the situation: it can boost morale and build up enthusiasm, people feel part of a larger whole, a variety of ideas and insights can be generated and many views and perspectives shared, more resources are available for implementing action, and so on.

Seating (p. 80)

Decide how the seating is best arranged, taking into account what people are used to, what will help them to participate and move easily into groups if necessary, and their need to see and hear each other and any overhead projector or chart you may use. You may need to explain why you have arranged the seating in a particular way.

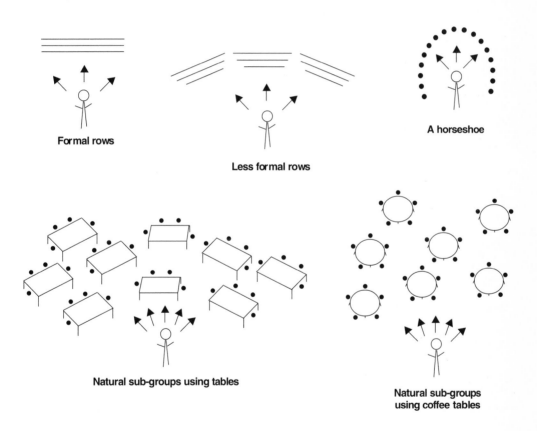

Formal rows

Less formal rows

A horseshoe

Natural sub-groups using tables

Natural sub-groups using coffee tables

Your introduction

On page 85 we discussed ways of opening a meeting. This is extremely important in large groups. It may be necessary to check that everyone can hear and see adequately.

In groups of twenty it may be possible for people to say who they are, but in larger meetings, it may help people to relax if given a few minutes to greet or introduce themselves to those they are sitting near.

Your delivery

It is harder to communicate with people in large numbers, therefore speak slowly and clearly, state things unambiguously and succinctly. It can help to repeat what you say in other words, and to use gestures, diagrams and visual aids (p. 66).

Structure and tasks (p. 49)

Keep the structure simple. Ensure people are utterly clear about what is expected of them at any one time (p. 44). Give clear instructions and write them up, check they are understood and acceptable. Allow enough time to do this adequately.

Participation

A variety of methods can be used:
- questions or tasks which members work at individually, giving them 2-15 minutes or more for this personal work;
- people talk to their neighbour or discuss in buzz groups thus obviating the need to move from the room for group work;
- sub-groups (p. 61) possibly with work sheets (p. 71);
- a role-play or playlet as a starter for discussion (p. 72);
- a panel who give their views and/or respond to discussion;
- extra breaks for people to relax, stretch, or chat. This is especially useful if people have become passive or sleepy.

The conclusion (p. 116)

The larger the group the greater the need to state clearly and check out any decisions and conclusions reached or yet to be worked on. Ensure, as far as possible, that people understand and are agreed about what action has to be taken and by whom.

3. **Groups of representatives**

Many people, representing several groups or organisations, come together to do business or work at a task together. There may be wide cultural, organisational and ideological differences between the members. Their participation is influenced by the reference group to which each is answerable. How can a facilitator make the most of this situation and avoid the pitfalls inherent in it?

Before a meeting

- Clarify, as far as it is possible to do so beforehand, the authority and responsibility of the group in decision-making (p. 44). What area of freedom will members have? Will they be able to negotiate a decision, subject to certain conditions or will they only be in a position to make a recommendation to the group they represent?

- Consider the various groups: What is the particular contribution of each? What are their special interests? What is each likely to want from the meeting, to be keen on, or to be uneasy about or to bring forward for discussion?

- Consider possible pitfalls which face you. These will depend on the relationship which exists between the groups. This could vary between co-operation and rivalry or faction. The representatives may be determined to outdo or outshine others or they may feel defensive or inadequate. The status of representatives may inhibit participation. There is also the danger of reaching unsatisfactory compromises or people being carried away by enthusiasm and making decisions which their organisation will not support.

- Consider the opportunities which face you. The potential influence and effect of such a group is enormous.

During the meeting

- In the introduction it is particularly important to assure members that their views and those of the groups or organisations from which they come will be respected and taken into account, and that undue pressure will not be brought on anyone or any group to fall into line. Highlight the value of having a group widely representative of many ideas and perspectives.

- Encourage people to remember the various groups or bodies from which they come. Give them time to check out how their organisation is likely to respond to ideas being put forward. This may mean a minute's pause in the meeting while they reflect or it may mean highlighting questions they need to ask their organisation between meetings.

- Do all you can to avoid individuals feeling trapped between the two groups, feeling that their own group is under censure, or being under pressure to agree or take action on something which makes them feel disloyal to their own group.

- Help members to understand and appreciate the position of each other's groups and organisations. Getting them to stand in each other's shoes may be appropriate (p. 74).

- It is vital to take time to explore any unease, objections, or questions, and mobilise the resources of the group to try and work out a way forward which takes these into account.

4. **Working with several groups**

You may find yourself invited to work with two or more groups or organisations which have come together for a particular task; for instance, voluntary agencies needing to work through a common problem; groups wanting to plan a programme of work together; or organisations uneasy about their relationship. Alternatively, you may be asked to work with one group to prepare its members to meet with another.

Before a meeting

Whether you are working with several groups together or preparing a group for a meeting with others, the complexity of the relationships requires thorough consideration beforehand. It is necessary to begin by clarifying the situation. Some of the information you may know (p. 39), but some of it you may need to seek from one or more of the parties concerned. Among the areas to be considered are the following:

(a) *The relationship between the groups*

However keen groups are to work together, potential difficulties are inherent in this situation. Each has built up its own identity, culture, way of communicating, and working, and these characteristics may not be understood or appreciated, at a conscious or unconscious level, by outsiders. What are the key characteristics of each group?

The groups may not be on equal footing, one may have more responsibility, power, ability or resources than the other. Is this the case with these groups? Is there a weaker party likely to need support? Is one group in a position of authority from which it is consulting the other?

The way the groups interact will depend to a large extent on their perceptions of each other, perceptions which may or may not be true to the situation. How do they see each other? Are they likely to threaten each other, become defensive, compete, close ranks, or to give in to each other too easily and paper over cracks?

Have they a history of working together, and if so, what is its legacy? What relationship do they want? What possible difficulties do you foresee?

(b) *The relationship between the facilitator and the groups*

Have you an existing relationship with any of the groups? What effect is this likely to have? How can you avoid being or being thought to be, partisan? (pp. 143 and 146).

(c) *Factors about the meeting itself*

Who has called or suggested the meeting? How enthusiastic are participants likely to be?

It is a routine or a special meeting? Is it one of a series or a one-off?

What is the reason for the meeting? What do they hope to achieve through it?

Is it to be held on the territory of one or other group or on neutral ground? Why has this been chosen? Could this venue pose any problems? If so, what can I do to overcome them? How can I help both groups to feel relaxed in the situation?

What opportunities does the meeting present? What is likely to help the groups to work together? What is likely to hinder them from doing so?

(d) *What preparation, if any, would be useful beforehand* (p. 78)?

What can you do to build up positive attitudes and expectations in the participants? Some of the ways outlined on page 41 for dealing with your own attitudes and feelings may suggest ways forward here.

Do you need to forewarn them about any difficulties they might face so they come prepared to work through them? If so, how can you do this in a way which challenges and motivates them? Clearly your own attitude towards the meeting will colour what you write to the participants.

What do you need to say about your stance and function and the way you will work (pp. 143 and 146)?

At the meeting

Some of the approaches and methods suggested below may, according to the circumstances, help to promote co-operation.

- Stress what all parties have in common (for example, their beliefs, values, attitudes, objectives for the meeting or desire to co-operate) and point out, as appropriate, what different contributions they each have to bring. Make it clear that working together on a particular task or making a joint decision, does not mean that they lose their separate identities or compromise their beliefs and values. I have found this important, for instance, when working with two organisations concerned with disablement who based their work on different theories; and in ecumenical discussion about co-operation where the denominations had very different beliefs and moral practices.

- Try to ensure that the benefits of co-operation are appreciated. One way is for you to list some of them, but it could be far more effective to set up an exercise of thinking or working together, through which people experience the richness of the other group and enjoy its company.

- Help groups to communicate: groups build up their own cultural identity and language and you may find you need to act as a go-between and to interpret one group to another. Ways of getting on to other people's wavelengths are described on page 107.

- Make opportunities for the sharing of necessary or useful information about each group. One method is for each group, on its own, to decide what information it wishes to share about itself and what it wants to know about the other(s). If the group is large, it could be helpful to form mixed sub-groups for the exchange of this information.

- Work for mutual understanding using suggestions on page 144.

- Where some problem is to be worked through some of the ideas on page 146 particularly the 'Two Rules of the Road' may be appropriate.

- Where only one group is present and is preparing itself to meet another, it can be useful to get members: to stand in the shoes of the other group (p. 74); to role play the introduction to the meeting or any particularly tricky issue which will be discussed (p. 72).

- The alternating use of homogeneous and mixed sub-groups can provide opportunities for people to explore new ideas and learn about other groups *and* to refer back to their own group at intervals (p. 61).

II PARTICULAR SITUATIONS

1. **Decision-making**[3]

Much already written has a direct bearing on decision making, but since this is so important and constant in the life of individuals and groups, this section is included. Matters dealt with earlier are only touched on here.

Decision-making can be simple or complex, spontaneous or long-drawn out, peripheral or crucial to growth and development. Some decisions are made for us, but the significant ones are those we make for ourselves, those only we can make. Other people may help us and we may help others. Below are some of the questions to ask in order to help a group, large or small, in a decision-making process about an important matter in which the facilitator may or may not be involved. The process may span a few sessions or be spread over several months.

Who is responsible for making the decisions?

You need to be clear and ensure the group is clear as to where the responsibility to make the decision lies. Is it with the group or are you engaged in a consultative process in which another group or individual in authority will make the final decision (p. 44)?

What kind of decision-making process does the group want to engage in?

Time taken in reaching agreement about the nature of the decision-making process which people want and to which they are prepared to commit themselves will pay dividends later. Various processes are described below. A group may decide on one or other of them or make its own amalgam or variation.

161

(a) *A democratic process.* Discussion is followed by voting in which the majority vote carries the day. In this it is necessary to agree on whether it is to be a straight majority or passed by some higher percentage. The chairperson may have a casting vote.

(b) *A consensus process.* This is usually seen as the ideal process but it has its dangers. One is that in working for unanimous agreement, individuals feel under pressure to go along with the majority for fear of holding things up interminably, or being seen to be 'the odd one out'. Working for genuine consensus can involve a great deal of time, energy and patience and a group using this path needs to be clear about that and committed to doing so.

(c) *A 'runyararo' process.*[4] This is subtly different from consensus. The term 'runyararo' , meaning 'for the good of the community', is borrowed from the Shona, who use it in settling disputes over which two parties cannot reach agreement through discussion. One of the two will eventually say with genuine commitment 'runyararo', that is, "for the good of the community I will go along with what the other party wants." It is not lightly arrived at. Working for 'runyararo' in decision-making recognises realistically that not everyone will feel the same about the outcome: some may be wholeheartedly enthusiastic, others moderately so, and some be prepared to live with it. If a vote is taken – and this is often called for in the constitution of a group – it allows individuals to vote against the decision favoured by the majority while committing themselves to fully support the outcome. The process leading up to this, if it is to be a genuine solution, is likely to require much time, energy and patience, but again, as with consensus, it makes for the unity and development of the group.

In presenting these alternatives to a group, help them to think about what each process realistically entails, their relative advantages and disadvantages and whether they are prepared to pay the cost. For instance, in (b) and (c) it is likely to mean spending a great deal of time exploring the reasons why some people are uneasy about what others see as the way forward, and being prepared to listen to fresh hesitations quite late in the day, when it looked as though all would be plain sailing. This is especially true of groups of representatives making decisions for a wider body of people not present (p. 157). For example, a group of thirty delegates representing several hundred members in a religious congregation had to decide whether or not to drop a certain traditional custom. Over a two week period the matter came up on numerous occasions; much time was spend in private reflection and discussion in small groups. On several occasions in the plenary session, having considered how some of the older members not present were likely to react, and having worked out compromises which everyone thought they would be able to accept with equanimity, someone would raise a further argument which those not present might put up, or even say, "I'm still uneasy, I have a niggle about this, can we look at it again?" The great advantage of this somewhat frustrating process, was that by the time agreement was reached, everyone felt able to explain the decision and the reasons behind it to the absent members, including those who were likely to find it most difficult to accept. And, in fact, the decision was subsequently accepted with very little hesitation by the rest of the congregation.

Other decision-making considerations

In discussing decision-making with a group it can be useful to consider such things as:

- Differentiating between making a decision, owning it and implementing it. All three are important and necessary parts if the outcome is to be fruitful.

- The time factor: if sufficient time is not taken in making a decision, you may find yourself spending an inordinate amount of time sorting out subsequent problems.

- The different ways in which corporate decisions affect individuals: some may find a decision harder to accept, some may be more involved in its implementation, some may bear more of the brunt or cost, some may be faced with greater difficulties as a result.

- The involvement of both head and heart in decision-making: it is not a purely rational process. At times one's thinking takes the lead and feelings need time to catch up; at other times one's feelings are in the ascendant and need to be thought about critically. In the best decisions, feelings and hunches are taken seriously and thought about rationally, alongside critical thinking about all other factors.

- Get a group to make a contract to commit themselves to staying with the process through any difficult periods, possible conflicts, confusion, or times of apparent stalemate. This can prove useful to encourage, motivate and challenge if and when such things occur (p. 94).

- The danger of 'Group Think': Irving Janis has coined this phrase to describe errors of decision-making based on group conformity thinking and misplaced loyalty to a leader or institution. The thinking of the group becomes 'frozen' and members resist outside pressure to re-examine their views. New information is ignored or used in such a way as to reinforce rather than challenge their stance. If this is a real danger in the group, a discussion about the phenomenon and the symptoms of 'Group Think' outlined by Janis and Mann could be useful beforehand.[5]

How will the decision be made?

One or two of the suggestions below may have been thoroughly discussed or merely touched on by the group when deciding on the nature of the decision. Not all that follows will be useful on all occasions and some suggestions are mutually exclusive. The question to ask yourself is: "What will be useful and acceptable in this particular situation?"

- *Setting the scene.* Relate the particular decision to its context, to the overall purpose of the group, and other significant factors, such as history and tradition, needs, problems and approaches. Consider why a decision is necessary now.

- *Agree on the purpose or objective behind the decision.*

- *Discuss and agree the time to be given to making the decision and consider what to do if time runs out.* A danger is to allow shortage of time to rush the group into making a decision, or to allow time-related factors to put pressure on people. For example, with a community building project, the longer the decision-making takes the higher the cost is likely to be. It is worth realising that if a decision is made before reaching genuine agreement on its future use, those involved may be storing up years of faction and frustration. The cost of going forward in a united, purposeful way is likely to be several thousand pounds. If put in this way, people may decide this is money well spent.

- *Work out the criteria.* How will possible ways forward be assessed? For example a local council agreed that their decisions had to "be of service to the local community" and "within so many thousand pounds"; a religious community agreed among other things that any decision had to "be in line with our mission statement" and "give priority to people on the margins of society". One danger is wasting time compiling a lengthy list of bland statements and generalities.

- *List all possible options.* Work out and list possible alternative ways forward or 'future scenarios'. Possibly stimulate people to think creatively by putting them into sub-groups or by having a brainstorming exercise. Some 'rules' of brainstorming are outlined on page 98. Whatever method you use assure people that individuals putting forward options will not necessarily be expected to be the one to carry them out, and that at this stage no suggestion will be ruled out of court.

- *Think through the options.* Some of the ideas below may encourage people to think objectively, critically and thoroughly about the various alternative proposals before them:

  – List the pros and cons of each. At times it may be useful to get those in favour to work on possible disadvantages and those against to focus on the advantages. Particular attention needs to be given to potential disadvantages: it may be possible to ameliorate them by amending or slightly altering the suggested proposal. Any final decision needs to take all the foreseen difficulties into account.

- Check proposals and suggestions for feasibility and realism. It is worth remembering the 'shift to risk' phenomenon by which groups are more likely to take risky decisions than are individuals. This can be advantageous but it also has its dangers.

- Get the members to stand in the shoes of the various parties who will be affected by the decision. For example, in deciding to close down a voluntary club, different members could feel their way into the thoughts and feelings of those who attend, the voluntary helpers, the paid staff and so on. Doing this will raise issues and questions which people may have overlooked (p. 74).

- Check that you have the necessary information and that it is accurate.

- Encourage people to raise anything they are uneasy or have questions about, and work through their thoughts and feelings with them. It can be in doing this that a minor but significant alteration is made to the decision. In one London church the design of the entrance was greatly improved after an elderly lady jibbed "at having to walk through all that open space".

- Clarify what will be expected of people if this or that decision is made: everyone may not be required to be as actively involved as others. For example, an American congregation of religious deciding about the Sanctuary Movement, avoided an impasse when it was clarified what would be expected of one member who, for various reasons, felt she could not be actively involved.[6]

- Get the group to work through each option in turn, as though they had decided on it, in order to help them think and feel their way through it. It can be difficult, but all the more important, to get people to do this in relation to alternatives they are not keen on. What effects will it have on whom? What do you feel about it? What possible difficulties will have to be avoided? How will others view this decision? What opportunities might it open up? How could it be implemented? Is this feasible in terms of time, ability, resources, money, etc.? Who will bear the brunt of the cost?

- Check that people are ready to make a decision. People take varying lengths of time to feel and think their way through things. It may be wise to fix a time limit within which to work but even then I would ask, "Are you ready to decide now or should we postpone the decision?"

I would usually add a caution against putting decisions off indefinitely. In deciding, we risk making a wrong decision but it can also be risky to delay decisions. I find groups need reassuring and encouraging on the one hand and a clear statement of the issues and what is at risk on the other.

- *Differentiate between the what and the how.* Although at times it may be advisable to work through how a particular alternative could be worked out, it can be useful to differentiate between *what* is being decided upon and *how* it will be implemented. Good decisions can be aborted by people saying "That can't be done", "We tried that and it didn't work." It can be that things have not worked in the past because the time was not ripe or because they were done clumsily. If a decision is the 'right' one, a way of implementing it can usually be found.

- *A discernment process.*[7] This is often used by religious groups but could be usefully adapted. It is based on the Ignatian model of prayerful reflection in order to discern the will of God. It can be used on its own, in preparation for discussion or in conjunction with it. The conditions necessary for discernment are that:
  - sufficient information is available with opportunity for questions. It is important to give time to this before the process begins;
  - a genuine commitment to being open to seeking what is best by way of a decision: this means avoiding argument or pressing for a particular alternative and being willing to change one's views if and when one becomes convinced.

The process itself has three threefold steps in relation to any particular way forward.

STEP 1: *Seeking the reasons **for** going a particular way*

(a) Everyone meditates privately about this in relation to the situation and circumstances and writes down their ideas.

(b) All return and share, by reading what they have written down, and listening. Depending on the size of the group this could be done in sub-groups. There is no discussion at this stage.

(c) Everyone goes off to reflect and meditate about what they have heard, and make further notes if they wish.

STEP 2: *Seeking the reasons **against** going in this way*

Follow the same threefold process as in Step 1.

STEP 3: *Weighing the reasons **for** and **against***

Follow the same threefold processes as above taking into account the reasons for and against.

Where sub-groups are used they may put their thoughts together and present them to the total group after Steps 1 and 2, or only after Step 3. Discussion follows. The process or part of it may be repeated at any stage.

- *Making provisional decisions.* Where a series of decisions are linked together or have to be made at the same meeting, it can release people's thinking to make a provisional decision about each issue in turn. After working through them, take time to return to the start and review how each decision now looks in the light of the later discussion and the other decisions.

- *Clarify areas of agreement and disagreement.* Have a series of 'straw votes' to give some indication of how much unease remains in the group. You need to be on the look out for what members are agreed about and where there are still areas of disagreement or uncertainty. It may be useful periodically to remind the group of the criteria and purpose on which they agreed at the start, and work from there towards a solution which honours these (p. 46).

How will the decision be implemented?

However 'good' a decision it remains barren if not implemented, and if badly implemented may cause harm. How it will be translated into effective action needs careful attention *while* the decision is being considered. Questions such as those below may well be woven into the decision making as it proceeds.

- What action needs to be taken? In what order? What needs to be done first?

- What can be done concurrently?

- When should it be started? Completed? It can be useful to make a flow chart of the work to be done in stages and with dates.

- Who will be responsible for carrying out the various aspects? Have they got the necessary skills and abilities? Do they need help or support of any kind, either from other group members or outside people or groups?

  If so, do they need any preparatory training? Have they the necessary resources or do we need to make arrangements to get them? Are we and they clear about their brief?

- What dangers or pitfalls do we need to avoid? Are there any safeguards we should build into the implementation?

- What is to happen if a problem arises? It can be useful to make contingency arrangements in case of crises or to prevent undue delays before people get stuck or into difficulties which they struggle with on their own. They may find it impossible to implement a decision, in which case they would need to report back and say why.

- Who is likely to be affected by our decision? When is the best time for them to hear about it? Should we share out some of the control we have by including them in the decision-making process and/or in deciding about its implementation? How are we going to tell them about the decision? Who will do this?

- When should progress be reported on and to whom? What should be done if the report is not forthcoming? It can be useful to work out some procedures so that a person or group is not waiting and wondering because they have heard nothing, and yet are afraid of appearing to interfere or check up if they enquire. When shall we review and evaluate our decision and its implementation?

2. **Short term withdrawal and re-entry**

We have considered what as a facilitator you must do *for* a group and what you must do *with* it in order to promote development. This section is about those times when it is advisable, necessary or expedient to withdraw and leave members to do things for themselves and *with* each other. It can be difficult to decide whether, when, and how to withdraw and to live with one's feelings afterwards. Such withdrawal may be temporary or permanent. This section concerns short-term withdrawal and re-entry.

Your withdrawal

There are times during a meeting when you withdraw to allow members to discuss or work at certain tasks on their own. What follows refers to withdrawal for several weeks or even for a period of months. Withdrawal may be necessitated by a sabbatical or a period of work elsewhere or you may not be needed while particular tasks are being worked on by the group.

It is important that any withdrawal is negotiated with the group. This will avoid misunderstanding, or members feeling let down or thinking you have lost interest. It also prepares for your re-entry. Mutual agreement and acceptance of the implications and possible consequences are crucial for the well-being of the group and your own peace of mind. The amount of negotiation will vary according to the situation. The factors below may need to be thought about by you as facilitator and it may be necessary to discuss some with the group:

- The potential benefits for you of withdrawing. Apart from having more time and space for yourself, other work or activities, it can be both salutary and encouraging to discover how well a group can function without you. To remain with a group can, at times, actually stymie development.

- Your motivation. Is it concern for the well-being of the group, to avoid a problem or to escape from a difficult situation? The latter may or may not be justified.

- The potential benefits for the group of your withdrawal. For example, is it likely to increase their self-confidence, their initiative or skills and abilities? Could it lead to less dependence? Might potential leaders emerge? Are they likely to feel freer to make a certain decision or to take a particular action?

- The possible dangers of withdrawing. Are they likely to become confused or angry? Will they fail in the task, lose their impetus, sense of security or direction? Will the group fall apart or end up in chaos? Are they capable of carrying on? Might one person dominate?

- Timing: when and for how long should you withdraw? How long will the next phase of the group's work last? Should a date for re-entry be arranged at this stage? Some of the factors considered below under *Your re-entry* might be usefully considered at this stage.

- The ability and motivation of the group to do what it has come together to do. For instance, have members the necessary skills, knowledge and resources? Will they allow and encourage their use? Can they get on with the plans made? Who will do what? If they need more help where can it be sought?

- The relationship between members. Are they likely to co-operate or compete? Is there a danger of in-fighting? Are relationships likely to be strengthened, weakened or broken? It can be useful to work out beforehand with the members what they will do if problems arise.

- The approaches and methods members are likely to use. Will they listen to each other, promote participation of everybody and take all views seriously? Or will they argue and put pressure on each other? Should they arrange for one or more of the group to act as facilitator?

- External relationships. Is there any danger of the group getting into conflict with another group or those in authority? Are members likely to dominate or pressurize other groups or individuals?

- Keeping in touch. Is any form of contact useful or appropriate during the withdrawal period? How would people feel if one or other party wants to make contact for any reason. For instance, the group, may realise it needs information or help, or you may feel uneasy about something or feel a need to know that all is well. Would a liaison person be useful?

Your re-entry

Both facilitator and group are faced with renewing their relationship. If the withdrawal has been for a number of months, much may have happened to both parties during the intervening period. Among the questions you might find it useful to ask yourself are the following:

- Have my purposes in relation to the group changed or developed?
- What are my objectives for the initial meeting?
- How can I get an accurate picture of what has happened in the group and where it now stands? Is a systematic review appropriate or a more informal conversation? What are the things I particularly want to know? How can I encourage members to tell me not just what went well but anything they are unhappy or uneasy about?
- Should we celebrate in any way? How can I express my pleasure both at being back and at any positive developments?
- How shall I respond if I find the group has lost ground, is in chaos or conflict, or I am uneasy about any decisions made or action taken?
- How can I share with the group what has happened to me and where I now stand?
- Am I in danger of pushing in and taking over unnecessarily?

3. **Permanent withdrawal**

Much of what has been written about short-term withdrawal is appropriate when you are preparing yourself and the group for your permanent withdrawal.

In permanently withdrawing from a group you may be handing over to one or more of the members or you may have a successor.

Any preparation needs to take into account your own position and feelings as facilitator or team leader, the group members and their feelings, your successor, if there is to be one, or how the group will continue on its own. These are dealt with separately.

The facilitator's preparation to withdraw[8]

Reflecting on the questions below may be done on your own or in conversation with a colleague. In either case you may find it helpful to write down your replies.

Reviewing your work with the group. What changes and developments have you seen in the way the group functions during the time you have worked with it? What are you satisfied/dissatisfied about? Have you any major concerns about withdrawing and handing over? If so, what are they? What could suffer in the transition?

Unfinished business. What unfinished business is there in relation to the work of the group? What difficulties remain? Are there any relationships within the group or between you and any members which need mending before you leave? Does anyone else need to be informed, for instance, other groups or individuals with whom the group is in touch?

Learning from your experience as facilitator. We can learn much from our previous experience. Often we say things like: "I'll never do that again." "In future I will make sure that. . . ." "That is something worth remembering." "I will never be the same after that." "That changes my approach to people/work/ things." Looking back what are the main things you have learnt from your work with this group which will influence your future thought and action?

Your feelings about leaving the group. What are your dominant thoughts and feelings about leaving? What are the advantages and disadvantages of leaving at this stage for you or for the group? Have you any strong feelings about any successor which you need to come to terms with?

What will you be leaving behind?

(a) Do a private brainstorm: jot down everything that you will be leaving: people, things and experiences.

(b) Read through what you've written and mark those things you are pleased to leave behind and those you will miss.

(c) Mark the things you need to do something about, to explain, to pass on, etc.

(d) Differentiate between what you will have to let go of and what you must or could maintain but in a new way.

(e) How are you going to let go of what you must let go of?

(f) How are you going to maintain what can be maintained?

Is there anything which will help to ameliorate your feelings? Dealing with one's feelings is discussed on page 41 and a brief exercise to help deal with negative feelings is given on page 42.

Preparing the group for your withdrawal

An early discussion about your withdrawal allows people to get used to the idea, to make any necessary decisions about the future, and to orientate to another way of organising themselves or to having another facilitator. It could provide a useful opportunity for review (p. 187). It may be useful to consider some of the points raised under *Short Term Withdrawal* on page 168. In addition opportunity might well be made for members:

– to express their thoughts and feelings and work through any difficulties they foresee and any negative feelings, especially if these are to do with their own inadequacy in facing the future without you. The various ways suggested on page 41 for working through your own feelings may be relevant when you try to help the group work through theirs.

– to decide about the future: how will they work? If there is to be no successor, how will they organise themselves?

Should they divide up the job of facilitator between them? Various people may be prepared to act as facilitator occasionally, or for a short period or do it with a partner. It is not always wise to rotate the job to all members, as some may simply not be good at it or find it extremely daunting and costly.

Should they divide up the various functions between them? For example, various people acting as convenor, timekeeper, introducing the discussion, keeping people to the point, doing any board work, summarising, etc. Some people may feel able to do one or other task, but not be responsible for all of them.

Preparing for your successor

Preparing adequately and positively for your successor can have a crucial effect on the well-being of the group and its future work. It can be useful, on occasion, to get members to stand in the shoes of your successor in order to empathise with his position before reflecting on the questions below (p. 74).

- If appointed, what do you know about your successor? Is he likely to use or be open to similar approaches and methods?

- Is there anything you and/or the group could do beforehand which would be helpful to him? Any information which could be sent? Are there any dangers in doing this?

- How and when will the group prepare to welcome your successor? What do they need to get across, say, or do at the first meeting in order to form a good working relationship?

4. Using outside expertise

A group may invite an outside expert or speaker to a meeting or series of meetings for various reasons, for example, because they want:

- to think more deeply about a subject or issue;

- to work through some programme, project or problem;

- to learn some skill or ways of doing something;

- to get information on a particular matter which it would otherwise take them too long to get or about which they need a technical explanation.

Outsiders may or may not benefit a group. Generally speaking they are more likely to contribute to the development process if the following questions have been considered before deciding to invite them:

- *Do the group members really want an outside expert or speaker?* To impose someone on a group can cause resentment which the outsider has to struggle to overcome. Worse still, the outsider could be seen as coming in to do something on behalf of a person in authority.

- *Are members clear and agreed about what they want an outside expert for?*

- *Are members able to do for themselves what they require of the outsider?* Further questions the group could ask itself are:

    Have we the necessary information, abilities, experience or skills?

    Do we need the objectivity an outsider brings?

    Would it be difficult or impossible for all of us to take part in the discussions and decision-making if one of us was facilitator?

Have we reached an impasse in which despite all our efforts we are unable to make progress?

Are we in conflict or faction?

Are we facing a particularly problematic or sensitive issue which we need to work through?

Before a meeting

Having decided to invite an outsider further questions need to be considered:

- How can we best brief her? Who will do so? The outsider needs:
  - to be clear about her brief and to find it acceptable;
  - to know why she is being asked in, the task which needs to be done, the overall situation and any relevant history, what the group knows or does not know, what thinking it has done or not done, and to be alerted to what is acceptable practice, what needs to be avoided and any danger signals or possible pitfalls. If she is to address certain questions, these are best given in written form;
  - to use approaches and methods consistent with those already in use or which the group finds acceptable or wishes to adopt.
- Who will brief her, when and how? This may be done in writing, on the telephone or a preliminary meeting may be necessary.
- Decide how to effect introductions between the outsider and the group. Would it help for each of the members to say a few words about themselves?
- Decide the respective responsibilities of yourself as facilitator, the outside expert and group members. Decide who will give a vote of thanks.

At the meeting

After the preliminary introduction you may hand over to the speaker for the entire meeting, or chair the question session or discussion. Unless the expert is used to handling discussions you would be wise to keep this in your own hands, in order to ensure ideas are considered as fully as possible and to stimulate active participation by the group.

When a speaker has been invited there are a variety of ways in which the period after the talk can be used:

- Give people time to formulate their questions, by having a coffee break, breaking into brief buzz groups, or dividing into sub-groups for a longer time (p. 61).

- Form 'listening teams'[9] beforehand. Each team listens with a particular aspect or question in their minds, for example: Which suggestions could we usefully try out? What is unlikely to work? What difficulties do we foresee? What ideas could we adapt? Each team will need time to put their ideas together before presenting them for discussion.

5. **Being a visiting expert**

The four sets of questions below may help you to decide whether or not to accept an invitation from a group to give a talk, facilitate a discussion or help in some other way. Other points made above may also be useful.

- *Am I clear about why they want me?* What do they want me to do? What are their expectations? Why have they asked me?

- *Am I able and willing to do this?* Is it something I have the skill and ability to do? Have I the necessary expertise? Will I be able to give the required information and ask sufficiently searching questions?

- *Do they really need me?* Could they do it for themselves? Am I in danger of colluding with them and undermining rather than building up their self-confidence and abilities? Could I help them more effectively in some other way?

- *Who is inviting me?* Does the group as a whole want me or am I being imposed on them by one member or a committee or someone in authority? Will I be seen as a spokesperson for those in authority? Have they been persuaded to invite me? Am I likely to be acceptable to the group?

If you decide to accept an invitation your contribution is more likely to be relevant and useful if you work on the questions below:

- *What background information do I need and how can I best get it?* A battery of subsidiary questions may be required in order to elicit the history, tradition, context, aims, atmosphere, situation, approaches, methods, practices, procedures, customs, theology, beliefs, values, assumptions, skills and abilities, ideas and feelings, etc. of the group and its members.

- *What is my purpose?* What do I hope to achieve in the lives of the group members? What effect do I hope to have? What do I want to happen as a result of my intervention?

- *Do I need to prepare the members in advance in any way* (p. 78)?

6. **Being a group member**

If you habitually use the approaches and methods described in this book it can be difficult and somewhat frustrating to be in a group in which the chairperson or leader is ineffectual or even directive. How can you apply these approaches as an ordinary member without appearing to take over or to criticise the way the situation is being handled? How can you promote systematic discussion of core issues without being seen as the person who always asks awkward questions?

If you belong to an on-going group, you know what to expect and can prepare before a meeting. Thinking about the problem when not immediately faced by it, is likely to help you take effective action when you find yourself unexpectedly in such a situation.

Before a meeting

Depending on the circumstances some of the following suggestions may prove useful.

- Explore the situation and your attitudes and feelings towards the meeting, the group and the chairperson or team leader. What do you find most difficult? What is likely to happen or not happen? Work through any negative feelings (p. 42).

- Work out your purposes or objective in relation to the meeting (p. 46). This can include the promotion of systematic and creative discussion.

- Identify any pitfalls you are likely to fall into and decide how you will guard against them and what you could do if you do fall into them.

- Decide what is of central importance for you in terms of the subject of the meeting. What issue really does need full discussion? If necessary, resolve to allow matters of lesser importance to be summarily considered.

- Ask yourself if there is anything you could usefully ask, say or suggest to the chairperson beforehand, for example, about a particular area or issue, about your part in the meeting, or by way of support. If the relationship is a good enough one assure him you want to help rather than hinder. It may be possible to agree that you will handle a particular issue or part of the meeting.

At the meeting

The following things may help you as a group member to promote systematic and creative discussion.

- Put your views and questions clearly and succinctly. While not talking at greater length than is necessary remember that to participate a lot is not necessarily unhelpful.[10] Use questions rather than make statements whenever appropriate. It can be useful to ask questions for clarification to help the discussion go deeper.

- Be tentative in your manner and careful in phrasing any intervention, especially when making suggestions, for example, "I wonder if it would help if we considered x" "It occurs to me it might be useful to. . . ."

- As appropriate, speak through the chairperson or leader, rather than address the whole group. Defer to the chair and avoid upstaging him.

- If you do take over at any point – and it may be useful to do so to clarify, summarise or draw a diagram – ask permission of the chairperson and hand back to him afterwards.

- Listen to other people and do what you can to ensure their points are taken seriously by commenting on them, building on them, asking questions to explore them or referring back to them at a later stage. Draw in other people who wish to speak, "I think X was about to say something" If you can, protect other members from criticism.

- Ensure you participate. This is particularly necessary if people know you usually have useful contributions to make. It can make people uneasy if you do not speak for a long time or look inscrutable.

- Make supportive and affirming comments and questions when you can do so in all honesty without appearing patronising. Avoid negative remarks or appearing over-critical.

- Test your own interventions. Strauss and Strauss[11] list some useful questions: "What will this question do to the discussion? Will it bring out something important. . . ? Will putting in this remark really help anybody see the problem from a different angle? If I give up arguing over this minor point, will it help to reach a decision?"

- Make your own notes if you can do so in an inconspicuous or acceptable manner. This may help you to produce a tentative summary or give some shape to the discussion.

- Avoid jargon and ask questions to clarify any terms used by others which may not be generally understood (p. 109). Questions for clarification can be useful.

7. **Terminating a group**

It is one thing to terminate a group which has been set up for a specific task or length of time, it is more problematic to decide that a group of long-standing has reached the end of its useful life-span. People are inclined to view the ending of such a group as a failure. In fact it may well be the right and courag-eous thing to do. In changed circumstances, with membership steadily shrinking, with no new recruits coming along, or where attendance becomes a burdensome duty, the question of closing down either temporarily or perm-anently makes good sense and is one members could well ask themselves. Success should not be equated with longevity.

The way in which a group is terminated can have a positive or negative effect on those involved, and build on or destroy much of the good which has been achieved. Various aspects need to be considered.

Maximising the value of what has been achieved

It could be important to review what has been accomplished by the group:

– in the lives of the members;
– in terms of work done and its effect on others whether in the organisation, local neighbourhood or further afield.

A report detailing the group's achievements might be drawn up for the members and possibly others who are implicated. Apart from listing them in the report, what could members do to ensure that any unfinished tasks or current work is handed on to other people? Is there room for a new group, possibly of younger people, to be formed from scratch?

Explaining the closure

For their own morale members need to be able to explain in a positive way that the time has come for the group to close down. Are there people outside the group who will be affected in some way and who may be disappointed or feel let down? How can they be helped to accept the closure with equanimity?

Dealing with the feelings of group members

Time needs to be given for members to talk about how they feel and come to terms with any feelings of disappointment or failure. Perhaps some sort of celebration would help the group to end with a bang rather than a whimper. Will members keep in touch in any way?

NOTES

1. See 'Meetings: Attending and Contributing to Them', a handout by George Lovell.
2. Kreeger Lionel *The Large Group* (Matesfield Reprints, H Kardack Books 1975).
3. Decision making is dealt with somewhat differently in Chapter Twelve 'Decisions and Decision Making' of *Small Communities in Religious Life: a practical guide for women religious* by Catherine Widdicombe (to be published in 2000).
4. I am indebted to Peter Russell who learnt of this as a missionary in Rhodesia (sic).
5. Irving Janis and Leon Mann *Group Think* (Collier MacMillan 1977).
6. 'Decision Making by Consensus' by Nancy Conway and Jean Alvarez in *Human Development* Vol. 9 No. 2 Summer 1988.
7. David Lonsdale SJ, *Dance to the Music of the Spirit* (Darton, Longman and Todd 1992).
8. This uses part of the 'Guidelines in Transition from One Job to Another', an Avec handout by George Lovell, in collaboration with Avec staff.
9. B. Strauss and F. Strauss *op.cit.,* p. 123. Note 18, p. 82.
10. H. Zelko in *Successful Conference and Discussion Techniques* (McGraw Hill 1957) points out that high participation is not necessarily disliked by other group members.
11. B. Strauss and F. Strauss *op.cit.,* p. 77. Note 18, p. 82.

PART SEVEN

Training oneself
and others

Developing one's skills comes through working with groups and reflecting on and learning from the experience. There is a natural flow from having a clearer understanding of the approaches described in this book; to developing one's skills and inducting others; to more formal training of oneself and other people. Overlap occurs all along the line. For the sake of clarity these various aspects are dealt with separately below.

I. BEGINNING TO WORK IN A NEW WAY

When beginning to work in a new way a golden rule is to go slowly and take small steps. This not only builds up your confidence and skills but is more likely to be acceptable to those with whom you are working. Working in the ways suggested below, you will assimilate new approaches and methods into your usual way of working; and gradually find yourself using them naturally and spontaneously. The following questions are intended to help you think about the best way to begin.

Preparation. Much has been said in Part Two about the need to prepare and ways of doing so. This is not repeated. Below are some additional factors for consideration as you start to change your customary ways of working (p. 35).

Your current practice. Consider your style and experience of working with groups: What are your strengths? What do you do well and feel confident about? How can you build on these things? What have you found works well? What does not work? What do you want to avoid?

Drawing on your experience. Use your experience to alert yourself to some of the pitfalls of working in new or unexpected ways with people:

*   How do I react when someone tries out something new on me?

*   What helps me to respond positively?

*   What puts me off?

Small safe steps. It is better to introduce innovations when there is sufficient trust between you and the group: people who do not know you can react adversely to finding the chairs in a circle instead of in the customary rows. There are some things which you can begin doing with safety, for instance, asking an open rather than a loaded question, and ensuring all contributions are taken seriously. You may find it helpful to focus on one skill at a time and to spend some time after a meeting checking up on how far you succeeded.

Explanations and requests. When you want to introduce something new or different it can help to ask permission and give a reason, so it is not seen as arbitrary (p. 186). "I wonder if I can use the board so we don't lose any of the points being made?" "It would help me if we could . . . , is that all right?" Or suggest trying something once to see whether it would work, "I've come across this way of tackling problems (p. 74), can we try it out and see if we find it useful?" It may be necessary to discuss your change of approach in order to avoid introducing the non-directive approach directively.

Responses to unhelpful comments. In his thesis on his work at Parchmore,[1] George Lovell devotes a chapter to the worker's responses to critical, sceptical and suspicious reactions to the non-directive approach and to people who were confused by it. This is described briefly in a recent book.[2]

All group workers are likely at some time to come up against someone who belittles or calls into question the way they work. Responding to such remarks, especially as they are often spontaneous and unexpected (pp. 115 and 116), can be difficult. However, they do provide opportunities for informal induction and can cause people to question what they are saying. Thinking through the sort of responses which could be made to negative or unhelpful comments, in addition to thinking afterwards what one could have said at the time, is a useful preparation for future occasions. One group, in half an hour, produced the following comments and various possible responses:

"We've always worked like this"

Responses: Do you find it always works? I wonder if we could think of any way of improving on it? Would it be worth just trying something out? Can I try something different to see if it works?

"We've tried that before"

Responses: Maybe the time was not ripe. How did you do it? Possibly the way it was done did not help. It could be useful to have another go and see if we can't make it work this time. Sometimes things work better a second time.

"Don't ask me to work like this"

Responses: Can you say what puts you off? Why do you feel like this? Have you ever tried?

"I don't like new methods"

Responses: I sympathise: most of us react against new methods at first. I wonder if we could discuss this? Could we just try it out and see whether or not it would be helpful?

"We haven't got all night!"

Responses: (taking this seriously) How long have we got? Is there time to do this or should we make a date to do it another time? We can't rush this, so what can we do?

"We need to be in control or else there'll be chaos"

Responses: What kind of control do you mean? Can we look at this because I don't want chaos either. What do we need to 'control' and what do we not want to control?

"Isn't this your job?"

Responses: As I see it, my job is to make sure it gets done in the most effective way, and I think we all need to be in on it if that is to happen. It's not something I can usefully do alone. Let's look at our respective contributions.

"That won't work!"

Responses: It's certainly difficult but can we have a go? What makes you say that? Have you ever tried it? Could we try it once and then assess it?

"You can try it"

Responses: I/we need your contribution too. It won't work as well if we aren't all working at it. What's putting you off? Why don't you want to be involved?

"That's their problem"

Responses: The way I see it, problems don't belong to anybody but all of us face them at some time or another. I wonder if it affects us in any way? Should we let them struggle with it on their own?

"We're happy as we are"

Response: Yes, but I feel really rather uneasy about it. I wonder if you would look at it with me?

One of the conclusions the group drew out was that people who 'block' in the various ways suggested above, are trying to reduce things and to sweep them aside. In taking them seriously, one is trying to expand and explore what is being said, to avoid snubbing people, and to challenge the underlying assumptions, so that people re-think what are often defensive clichés.

II. ENCOURAGING GOOD PRACTICE IN OTHERS

Using the approaches advocated in this book with a group over a period of time, is one way of informal induction, so that people not only use them in the group in which you are working, but adopt them themselves when working with other groups. More formal training courses are discussed on page 193. This section describes some practical and proven ways of encouraging good practice in others. They vary from the *ad hoc* to a more systematic approach. It is up to you to decide what will best fit you and any particular group with which you are working.

Explain what you are doing and why. Giving some explanation of the theory underlying your practice has been mentioned on page 184. Working out and articulating a straightforward explanation is a useful discipline which makes you question what you are doing and prevents you from unthinkingly adopting a method from another person or situation. The explanation may be given beforehand or afterwards, or the value of it may be discussed, through asking people how they found doing such and such. With more erudite groups your explanation may be backed up by putting it in more technical terms and quoting your sources. Brief written explanatory papers or handouts, varying from the simple to the more academic, could be offered to group members for their private reading or as a basis for a later discussion.

Answer questions. Encourage people to ask questions which you can use as opportunities for informal education into co-operative ways of working. At times you may give a factual reply, at others it may be more productive to suggest people pause "so we can all think about this". This practice is likely to make for increasingly thoughtful and critical participation from which you and others will learn.

Introduce discussion about different approaches. One way of doing this,[3] is to distinguish three different ways of working:

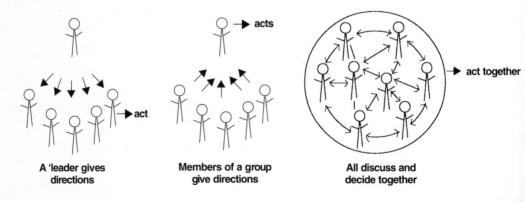

A 'leader gives directions   Members of a group give directions   All discuss and decide together

There are pros and cons to each approach, and each can be appropriate in different situations at different times. In three groups, members could explore a different approach and share their ideas as to its strengths and weaknesses with the others. Such a discussion would avoid the danger of imposing an approach on a group.

Evaluate how things went. A single meeting or event, a series of meetings, or the performance of the group in general, may be evaluated and, as has already been said, this may be done informally and in general terms (p.126) or more detailed questions about the different parts of the discussion can be considered. Feedback can be encouraged by your openness to questions and criticisms, and your readiness to admit mistakes. None of us can claim to be faultless facilitators: human beings and situations are too complex and we all have our weaknesses as well as our strengths. An undefensive attitude can lead to stimulating and enlightening discussion which becomes a learning experience for all concerned.

Various methods of evaluation are suggested below, some more formal than others.

- Get the group to consider the questions which need to be asked to assess how the meeting went. List and order the questions and then tackle them together. It can help to suggest that critical points are made in a way in which they can most easily be handled. For instance rather than saying, "Some people never contribute and I feel they're silently disapproving", you could say, "I find myself interested in knowing what people are thinking, and sometimes I'm not sure whether they're approving or disapproving."

- A similar but more focused question would be to ask people to reflect on the meeting and to jot down (a) the kind of contribution which they found most useful and which helped them to engage in an inner dialogue; and (b) the kind of contribution which closed them up, made them feel defensive or prevented them from thinking openly. This could be done as a private exercise, shared in pairs or small groups; or discussed all together if people feel able to be open enough. It could be a significant exercise for the group, as it draws attention to the quality of people's interventions and it is this that makes for a real meeting of minds and hearts.

- Ask the members to identify 'the difficulties we face in our meetings' and then tackle them, possibly by using the problem tackling sequence (p. 74).

- More formally, members could address a series of questions similar to those suggested on page 119. Use of a work-sheet could be helpful (p. 71).

- Members could check their performance, privately, in pairs or sub-groups, or as a full group against any ground rules or code of good practice (p. 189) they have formulated.

- The characteristics of a good group or team suggested by someone else could be used to check your way of working together. For instance, Peter Ribotto's[4] top team developed the criteria below as 'characteristic of an ideal team' and used them to evaluate the team effectiveness.

'Requirements for team effectiveness:

- Select right team, with each member understanding limits of jurisdiction.

- Possess basic technical competence.

- Possess analytical ability.

- Candour: ability of team members to express and accept.

- Ability to ignore status differences in discussions.

- Ability to draw out and respect contribution of each team member, by good listening or actively encouraging participation.

- Let leadership and control of direction evolve naturally within constraints of time and relevance.

- Attempt consensus decisions and total commitment; failing that, have a strategy for decision-making that insofar as possible achieves participation and commitment.

- Each team member accepts responsibility for management of time.

- Willingness to listen to doubts, hunches, intuitions, innovations.

Preventing effective teams:

- Individual desire to win own points, impress other members.

- Wandering, irrelevancies, no team discipline.

- Laughing at, putting down people.

- Insistence on status in decision-making – excessive deference to status.

- Oblivious to outside constraints.'

- Get the group to work out what *they* think makes for a good group or team work. Alternatively, they could articulate and discuss their own strengths and weaknesses as a group and how to build on the one and overcome the other.

- Suggest members spend ten minutes at the start of a meeting identifying 'what to avoid' and ten minutes at the end asking themselves, "Did I/we avoid them?"

Alert people to good practice. One simple procedure for doing this is to ask each member to jot down one or two things which help them to participate in a meeting, and one or two things which hinder them from doing so. Each person then reads out what they have written, first on the positive side and then the negative. From this a more formal code of good practice for the group could be drawn up. This can be added to periodically. Doing this is particularly useful when a worker wants to help a group, which does not function well to improve its performance. It gives members an opportunity to stand back and reflect on how they both help and hinder each other. It could be a useful review meeting in itself.

Develop listening skills see (p. 105)

Use check lists. A check list of questions which members can ask themselves before or during a meeting could be drawn up by the group or individually. For a list drawn up by Lovell, see page 153 and questions suggested by Strauss and Strauss, see page 177.

Work in tandem. To ask one or two members of the group to prepare a meeting or event with you, can prove a useful training opportunity. By inviting different individuals you could eventually have included most or all of the group. Having helped to prepare a meeting, a member could be asked to make a check list to ensure certain points are raised, or take a more active co-worker role (p. 95), or facilitate part or the whole of the meeting while you support them as co-worker. Thinking through these progressive stages in relation to different individuals can be important. To get someone to attempt more than they are able to do, can lead not only to a disastrous meeting but to eroding self-confidence, which may take a long time to re-establish. Gradually increasing a person's responsibility and extending their skills is invaluable training.

Use of case study. This has been described on page 128 under '*Coping with failure*'. Cases can be useful learning exercises for people in an organisation or in a community.

III. ONGOING SELF-TRAINING

The ways of working described in this book are of proven value in promoting development both of facilitators and those with whom they work. This section focuses on your own development: how you can work in such a way that you become increasingly competent and confident as you work and what supplementary activities will promote your self-training. This process of assimilating new ideas and approaches so that they become part of you and your way of working requires time and effort.[5]

Learning to think

Not surprisingly, the quality of a group's thinking at a meeting is likely to reflect the quality of the facilitator's thinking beforehand. If you are able to think clearly, deeply, systematically, laterally, critically, openly and creatively you are in a better position to help others to do so. Learning to think is therefore key to one's own development as a facilitator.

We each need to do our own thinking if we are to internalise ideas, deal with our feelings, make use of our experience, come to new insights, and make those decisions which no one else can make for us, about how we respond or react to the ups and downs of life and death. Although thinking is natural to us, something we have always done, the pace and complexity of modern society does not encourage the deeper, more reflective thinking necessary for wisdom and maturity. Neither is it always easy or comfortable to think creatively: it can be exacting, demanding and challenging.

One way of learning to think more effectively is to work close to someone who is a systematic and thorough thinker: an option not open to everyone. Edward de Bono has written several books on the art of thinking.[6] This book itself has been written with the intention of stimulating the reader to reflect critically and openly on the ideas and suggestions put forward. Working on any of the following questions may help you to explore your own thinking skills and abilities, in order to learn from and build on them when trying to help others to think. Work on those questions which appeal to you or stimulate you.

What should I be thinking about? Try to identify those things which are important in your life and which need to be thought through, even though such thinking can be a painful process. Are there things I consistently avoid thinking about? Why do I not want to think about them? Am I afraid to? Why? Do I think these things are important to me? Do I believe I should think about them? What escape routes do I use to avoid thinking about them? Can I remember times when someone has tried to get me to think about something which I was not concerned about or did not want to think about? What happened and why? What did they do and what did I do? How do I explain this to myself?[7]

What hinders or prevents me from thinking? Some of this may already have been covered. How do I hinder or prevent myself thinking or justify not thinking? How do others hinder or prevent me? How do circumstances and the situation I am in hinder me? What have I learnt about helping myself to avoid, ameliorate or overcome these difficulties?

What helps me to think creatively? When have I thought creatively? What helped me to do so? What effect do the following have on my motivation and ability: the questions I ask myself or am asked, the time of day, the place, being alone or thinking with others, other people, sound, comfort, preparation, orientation, writing, other activities? What have I learnt about helping myself to think?

Finally jot down a few of the most important insights which are relevant to your work of facilitation and which you have gained from the above exercise.

Self-training as you work with people

The actual working situation offers great potential for learning and increasing your skills. Some ways in which this can be done have been outlined earlier. They are included for easy reference.

- Identify your learning needs: jot down those things which you need to strengthen up, this could be to do with asking searching questions (p. 56), listening (p. 105), being more tentative, using diagrams (p. 66) or not putting undue pressure on people. Raising your awareness of a skill in this way can alert you to its use when the need arises or you could work at them one at a time.

- Evaluate your work (p. 126). It is useful to book time in your diary not only for a meeting and its preparation, but also to assess how it went. The occasional 'away day' to read over and reflect on what you are learning will contribute to your own development as an effective facilitator.

- Tackle problems as they occur using the problem-tackling sequence (p. 74).

- Write up a 'case study' of a fiasco or failure and working through it alone or with a colleague (p. 129).

- Write a structured record of a meeting: the value of this as a way of developing your skills in face-to-face work is described on page 123.

- Write up your work with a particular group: trace the various stages of its development and identify what led to them; describe any difficulties and what you did which ameliorated or overcame them. Through researching your work in this way, you not only contribute to your own learning but make what you have learnt available to others[8].

Co-learning

Facilitators and co-workers are in a position to learn together by discussing how a meeting went (pp. 126 and 131). This may be done more systematically if you have a colleague who will partner you as facilitator and observer in turn. Being observed as you work, and observing your partner, and having a discussion afterwards, on a regular basis, is an invaluable learning experience[9]. Further practice can be provided in a 'sheltered' situation on a training course (see *Courses* p. 193); or perhaps by a group of colleagues taking turns at leading a discussion among themselves, followed by an assessment of what the facilitator did which was helpful and what was unhelpful.

Observing

It can be useful to observe and assess how other people lead groups, whether actual groups of which one is a member or groups on TV.

As an observer, focus on what the facilitator does or does not do to help or hinder the discussion, keeping in mind both the systematic flow of ideas and the way in which people are participating. Observing is a skill in itself[10] and the observer may find it useful to have a check list or to focus on one or more particular aspects such as:

- the facilitator's questions: see *Question and Questioning* (pp. 55);

- the methods used (p. 66), for example, visual aids, the drawing of diagrams, board work, etc.;

- those things which either aid or block communication (p. 105);

- participation of the group as a whole: what galvanises the group and what the facilitator does when the group is passive (p. 135);

- participation of individuals: what the facilitator does to encourage everyone to participate, how she deals with people who dominate (p. 138) and the silent members (pp. 93 and 135);

- structuring the discussion: what structure does the facilitator introduce at the start of the discussion, how rigid or flexible is she in its use? What structure does she draw out of the discussion as it goes along (p. 49)?

Reading and Reflection

Some useful books on group work are mentioned in the Bibliography. To get the most from what you read it can help:

- to take notes;

- to annotate the text;

- to make yourself an index of things you may want to refer to;

- to develop a card reference system under various headings and note references for different books or articles, ensuring you have title, author, publisher and date of publication;

- to take photocopies and develop a filing system which matches your card index. Working systematically at this can build up a rich resource of useful material.

Courses

Participation in a course can be a boost to one's on-going self-training. Many courses are offered on group work or on allied subjects. To identify clearly what you are seeking to learn and to consider whether or not a particular course is offering it, can save much waste of time and money. If the information given on a brochure is insufficient, most course directors will welcome a telephone conversation to ask questions about content, approach and method, participants, and things such as depth, level, and scope. It can be frustrating for all concerned, when people attend a course which does not match their needs. Courses focusing specifically on the non-directive approach to group work are conducted by the author.[11]

In order to make the most use of a particular course, identify for yourself what you want to get out of it and how you will participate. For example, would it help to take full or brief notes? Are you likely to re-read or use them in any way? Too often notes are filed away and gather dust. Could you spend a short time each evening clarifying what you have learnt during the day either from formal talks and explanations, or from experiencing or observing the process? Decide, towards the end, what use you will make of what you have learned. Would it help you to put a review date in your diary, when you will consider a certain point or review what you have decided to do or simply to re-read the notes? Are there particular ideas or insights you hope to pass on to a colleague or to any group with which you are working?

IV CONCLUSION

Working with communities and organisations for human and spiritual development must entail some work, and often quite a lot of work, in small groups. As I have indicated in various places throughout this section, becoming skilled in working non-directively is not an easy option, but it is a worthwhile one. When I myself came across the approaches underlying this book, I felt liberated. My confidence grew as I came to realise both in theory and practice, the rich resources which were available in those with whom I worked. I can only hope that you who use this book will also have satisfying and rewarding experiences as you work.

NOTES

1. *An Action Research Project to Test the Applicability of the Non-Directive Approach in a Church, Youth and Community Setting* (Unpublished doctoral thesis, Institute of Education, London University, 1973).
2. *The Parchmore Partnership: George Lovell, Garth Rogers and Peter Sharrocks* edited by Malcolm Grundy (An Avec publication 1996).
3. I learnt this from seeing it used by George Lovell.
4. Unfortunately I cannot now trace where this is from.
5. Researching the use of these approaches in church and community work over thirteen years led me to conclude that to assimilate them so that they become an habitual way of working requires both theological reflection and on-going help and support. *The Roman Catholic Church and Vatican II: Action Research into Means of Implementation* (Unpublished thesis for an M. Phil, Institute of Education, University of London 1984, pp. 186-289). Their skilled use in group work is simple but not without effort.
6. See *The Five Day Course in Thinking* by Edward de Bono (Penguin 1967) and other books of his listed in the Bibliography.
7. I am indebted to Peter Lang of the Kensington Consultation Centre (London) and George Lovell for some of these questions which they developed for a joint Avec/Westminster Pastoral Foundation course in 1986/87.
8. George Lovell 1973 *op.cit.*, p. 56 Note 1.
9. This is how I began using these approaches in 1968 in co-operation with John V. Budd, a neighbouring vicar.
10. T.R. Batten 1967 *op.cit.*, p. 120 Note 1 p. 22. Strauss & Strauss *op.cit.*, p. 39 Note 18, p. 82 outline the task of a group observer, and conduct of a subsequent discussion about the way the group worked. Rob Brown and Margaret Brown in *Empowering Leadership* (Nicholas Brealey 1994) have a useful 'Brief for Observers of Group and Team Discussions', p. 20.
11. Catherine Widdicombe, The Grail, 125 Waxwell Lane, Pinner, Middx HA5 3ER.

Selected bibliography

Committees

Clarke, Steve *Working on a Committee* (Community Projects Foundation 1980)

Cowper, Geraldine Sayers *The Write Stuff: Effective Minutes and Agendas: A Major Video Training Programme* (The Industrial Society Press 1991)

Headley, Rodney and Rochester, Colin *Understanding Management Committees: A Look at the Volunteer Committee Members* (Volunteer Centre, 29 Lower Kings Road, Berkhampstead HP4 2AB 1992)

Locke, Michael *How to Run Committees and Meetings: A Guidebook to Practical Politics* (Macmillan Press 1980)

Scottish Council for Voluntary Organisations *Training Work Pack: Committees* (SCVO, 18-19 Claremont Crescent, Edinburgh EH7 4QD))

Walton Roger L, (Ed) *It's More than Sitting in the Chair* (Methodist Church Division of Ministries 1993)

Conflict

Coser, Lewis *The Functions of Social Conflict* (Routledge and Kegan Paul 1972)

Fisher, Roger; Ury, William and Patton, Bruce *Getting to 4 – yes: negotiating agreement without giving in.* (Hutchinson 1990, c1981)

Janis, Irving and Mann, Leon *Decision Making: A Psychological Analysis of Conflict, Choice and Commitment* (Collier MacMillan 1977)

Livingston, Donald 'Rules of the Road' *Personnel* Jan/Feb 1977

Lorenz, Konrad *On Aggression* (Methuen 1966)

Storr, Anthony *Human Aggression* (Pelican 1974)

Worsley, Jenyth and Wheen, Natalie. *Learning to win: negotiating – your way.* (Careers and Occupational Information Centre, Sheffield, 1988)

General

Amadeo L and Gill J S 'Managing Anger and Hostility' *Human Development* Vol. 1 No 3 Fall 1980

Batten, T R *The Human Factor in Community Work* (Oxford University Press 1965)
The Human Factor in Youth Work (OUP 1970)
The Non-Directive Approach in Group and Community Work (OUP 1967) Abridged version *The Non-Directive Approach* (An Avec Publication 1988)

Benson, Jarlath. 1991 *Working more creatively with groups* (Routledge 1991)

Bertcher, Harvey *Group participation: techniques for leaders and members* (Sage Publications 1994)
and Maple, Frank *Creating groups* (Sage Publications 1996)

Bono, Edward de: *The Five-Day Course in Thinking* (Penguin 1967)
Future Positive (Maurice Temple Smith 1979)

Bradford, Leland P *Making Meetings Work: A Guide for Leaders and Group Members* (University Associates USA 1976)

Brown, Allan *Groupwork:* (Arena 1992)

Brown, Rob and Brown, Margaret *Empowering Leadership* (Nicholas Brealey 1994)

Buzan, Tony *Using Your Head* (BBC 1982)

Cohen, Anthony P (Ed) *Symbolising Boundaries: Identity and Diversity in British Cultures* (Manchester University Press 1986)

Conway, Nancy and Alvarez, Jean 'Decision Making by Consensus' in *Human Development* Vol. 9 No 2 Summer 1988

Crimmens, Paula. 1998 *Storymaking and creative groupwork with older people* (Jessica Kingsley 1998)

Dillistone, F W *The Power of Symbols* (SCM Press 1986)

Douglas, Tom *Basic groupwork.* (Routledge 1988)

Douglas, Tom *A Handbook of common groupwork problems* (TavistockRoutledge 1991)
A Theory of Groupwork practice (Macmillan Press 1993)

Dwivedi, Kedar Nath *Group work with children and adolescents: a handbook* (Jessica Kingsley 1993)

Edwards, Betty *Drawing on the Right Side of the Brain* (Fontana/Collins 1979)

Egan, Gerard *You and Me: the Skills of Communicating and Relating to Others* (Brooks Cole USA 1977)

Fromm, Erich *To Have or To Be* (Jonathan Cape 1978)

Gibson, Andy. and Clarke, Gaynor *Project-based group work facilitator's manual: young people, youth workers and projects.* (Jessica Kingsley 1995)

Gill, James 'Indispensable Self-Esteem' in *Human Development* Vol. 1 No 3 1980

Gordon, Esther *Wholetime: A Handbook for Workshops* (A Grail Publication 1996)

Grundy, Malcolm (Ed) *The Parchmore Partnership: George Lovell, Garth Rogers and Peter Sharrocks* (Chester House Publications 1994)

Habershaw S & T and Gibbs, G *53 Interesting Things to do in your Tutorials and Seminars* (Technical and Educational Studies Bristol 1987)

Janis, Irving and Mann, Leon *Group Think* (Collier MacMillan 1977)

Kaplan, Allan *The development practitioners' handbook* (Pluto Press 1996)

Kreegar, Lionel (Ed) *The Large Group* (Maresfield Reprints, H Karnack Books 1975)

Lewis, Byron and Pucelik, Frank *Magic Demystified: A Pragmatic Guide to Communication and Change* (Metamorphous Press 1982)

Lonsdale, David *Dance to the Music of the Spirit* (Darton, Longman and Todd 1992)

Lovell, George *An Action Research Project to Test the Applicability of the Non-Directive Concept in a Church, Youth and Community Centre Setting* (Unpublished doctoral thesis, Institute of Education, University of London 1973)
Diagrammatic Modelling: An Aid to Theological Reflection in Church and Community Work (William Temple Foundation Occasional Paper No 4 1980. Reprinted as An Avec Publication 1991)
Analysis and Design: A Handbook for Practitioners and Consultants in Church and Community Work (Burns & Oates 1994)
Ministry Through Consultancy: A Handbook for Work and Vocational Consultors and Consultants in Christian Organizations (Burns & Oates 2000)
Avec: Agency and Approach (An Avec Publication 1996)
The Church and Community Development: An Introduction (Grail Publications and Chester House Publications 1973 Reprint by Avec Publications 1992)
(Ed) *Telling Experiences: Stories About a Transforming Way of Working with People* (Chester House Publications 1996)
and Widdicombe, Catherine *Churches and Communities: An Approach to Development in the Local Church* (Search Press 1978, reprint 1986)

Mackay, Ian *A Guide to Asking Questions* (British Association for Commercial and Industrial Education 1980)

Maskell, Pauline: *Working in Groups: a quick guide* (Daniels Publishing 1995)

Mello, Anthony de *Sadhana: A Way to God* (Image Books, Doubleday NY 1984)

Morgan, Gareth *Images of Organisations* (Sage Publications 1986)

Morris, Desmond *Manwatching: A Field Guide to Human Behaviour* (Jonathan Cape 1977)

Mullender, Andrey and Ward, Dave *Self-directed groupwork:users take action for empowerment* (Whiting and Birch 1991)

Napier, David: *Organising Conferences and Events: a quick guide* (Daniels Publishing 1995)

Petrie, Pat *Communicating the Kingdom: Communication Skills for Christians* (Grail Publications 1992)

Progoff, Ira *At A Journal Workshop* (Dialogue House Library NY 1975) *Process Meditation* (DHL 1980)

Ramsey, Ian T., *Models and Mystery* The Whidden Lectures for 1963 (Oxford University Press 1964)

Rico, Gabriele Lasser *Writing the Natural Way: Using Right-Brain Techniques to Release Your Expressive Powers* (J P Tavener, Houghton Miffin 1983)

Sandford, John *Burnout* (Paulist Press 1982)

Schindler-Rainman, Eva and Lippitt, Ronald in collaboration with Jack Cole *Taking Your Meetings Out of the Doldrums* (University Associates USA 1975)

Schuon, Donald *Beyond the Stable State* (BBC 1971)

Strauss, Bert and Strauss, Frances *New Ways to Better Meetings* (The Viking Press 1957)

Watzlawick, Paul, Weakland, John and Fisch, Richard *Problem Formation and Problem Resolution* (W W Naughton 1974)

Widdicombe, Catherine *The Roman Catholic Church and Vatican II: Action Research into Means of Implementation* (Unpublished thesis for Degree of Master of Philosophy, Institute of Education, London University 1984)
Small Communities in Religious Life: A Practical Guide for Women Religious (To be published in 2000)

Wink, Walter *Transforming Bible Study* (SCM Press 1980)

Zelko, Harold P *Successful Discussion and Conference Techniques* (McGraw Hill 1957)

Index

Several of the terms below will make little sense to you before reading particular sections of this book. However, I have included such terms because, once read about, you may later search for them. This index aims to help you in such a search. My basic intention has been to include items to which readers are likely from time to time to want to refer. Where appropriate, when several page numbers are included under one heading, the main numbers are emboldened.

Index of Names